Pickles' Parables

Lessons Learned From a Beagle

Diane R. Brown
Renelynn Publishing

United States of America

D1157904

Published by Renelynn Publishing
picklesparables@gmail.com

ISBN 978-0-578-56611-5
Cover design: Renelynn Publishing
Interior design: Renelynn Publishing
Photos: Diane Brown
Illustrations: Chloe Calhoun

Printed in the United States
Copyright 2020

Mark 16:15
And He (Jesus) said to them, "Go into all the world and
preach the gospel to every creature"
...and God sent forth a beagle.

In Memory
Paul L. Mesplay

My earthly father who gave me my first beagle and who loved to hear the musical "Baroo" of a beagle in hot pursuit of a rabbit.

Proverbs 20:7

The righteous man walks in his integrity: His children are blessed after him

Dear Heavenly Father,

I pray Your hand upon this book, Pickle's Parables. The book You have laid upon
my heart to write. I pray that not one word go in that is not from You and not one
word be left out that needs to be included. For You, dear Lord already know the hands
that will pick it up and the eyes that will read the pages. I pray for each and every one
that reads Pickles' Parables, that God, You will provide what is needed in their life
according to Your divine wisdom. Humbly and sincerely prayed from my heart.

Amen

Prologue

The writing of "Pickles' Parables" has been a spiritual journey for me as well as a time of spiritual growth. It has been a lesson in being patient and waiting upon the Lord and His perfect timing. I pray each and every chapter will be an inspiration to you. To that person who may be struggling to be obedient to what God is asking from you, something you feel you are not capable of, or perhaps it is something that you feel isn't even humanly possible, I agree. Some things just are not possible no matter how hard we try. However, if God is calling you for a particular task, it can and will be accomplished if you allow God to have control. With God ALL (not some) things are possible.

Matthew 19:26
But Jesus looked at them and said to them, "With men this is impossible, but with God all things are possible."

Genesis 1:1
In the beginning God created the heavens and the earth.

God is the creator and has dominion over all things, great and small. God is above satan. For this reason you will notice in my writings God's name is capitalized as well as any references to Him. satan's name is not capitalized, even when his name is at the beginning of a sentence.

My God, the one and only true God, is worthy of praise and the upmost respect that I am able to offer up to Him.

Revelation 1:11
I (God) am the Alpha and the Omega, the First and the Last.

Thank You's

First off let me say that I wrote and edited this one page all by myself. If there are grammatical or punctuation errors on this page, which I am fairly certain there are, please do not blame my editors. They did not get to see this page until the book was published. This was my one chance to write what I wanted without being chastised or reprimanded, allowing me a sense of freedom sprinkled with a spirit of rebellion. You can bet your grandma's biscuits that my editors are reading this and groaning in their grits about now.

As a fair warning to you the reader, if you are an English major or minor and subject to gastrointestinal upset due to grammatical errors, it might be a good idea to skip the rest of this page.

No book is complete without thanking those who played an important role in getting a finished product that is not a total embarrassment to all mankind. Writing a book is easy, it is all those other pesky little details that can drive a person stark raving mad, more specifically, the author (me), who teeters on the edge most of the time anyway.

Number one to thank would certainly have to be the husband, aka Mr. Brown, because I live with him, and he is my team mate. Mr. Brown not only believes in me but was, and still is, my greatest encourager. Of course he's also financially responsible, becoming the sole Brownstead breadwinner when I quit work to finish the Pickles' Parable project. Beyond believing in me, Mr. Brown listened to God's prompting, stepping forth in faith, and obedience, when he knew the road we were about to take would have pot holes and other obstacles along the way. I can't think of anyone I would rather go through life's pot holes with than Mr. Brown.

My two editors, who were put to the test and passed. I did sense some frustration on their part, with my kindergarten wording and lack of appropriate use of ,?":;!. Were it not for Julie and Sarah, there would be many of you who would suffer from psychological trauma caused by my grammatical errors. The editor's diligence and attention to detail (I referred to it as nit picking) hopefully circumvented any permanent psychological damage to sensitive individuals.

Julie Mesplay's many years of successful writing, reviewing, and working with classified government documents at a high level made her a natural at editing. She can spot a spacing error from across the room with the lights turned off and questioned why I could not see what was in plain sight. Apparently extra spaces glare at her with a menacing look, but merely smile at me, leaving me with a false sense of security and that all is well. Julie is an amazing woman that gives so much of herself to all those around her, always willing to step in to fill the gaps and tackle the hard projects. Never afraid of hard work or challenges. Jewells (as I affectionately call her) also sent shipments of high octane coffee to keep me going, going, and going..........Jewells a rare but true gem.

Sarah Calhoun, the comma queen, with a love and passion for comma's which I do not have, I barely like comma's. Bless her heart, I'm sure she suffered many sleepless nights worrying about the lack of comma's in God's book. I am thankful for her ability to see what needed to be put where. In spite of a difficult year for her, she read, reread and edited, making suggestions in sentence structure to help improve the flow of the book. She also happens to be my favorite first born, who has a tender heart, and a love for helping others. Did I mention she is an awesome mom to 4 of the cutest, sweetest, smartest, and best little people that I know? These, commas, are, just, for, you, Sarah,.

Chloe Calhoun, my lovely illustrator who decided to throw in a broken arm to delay the illustrations. Bumps, bruises, and broken bones are just some of the hazards of hiring a ten years old illustrator. Pickles' Parables has always been in God's timing, so what's a broken bone here or there. Whatever I asked of Miss. Chloe she was able and willing to draw. Capturing the perfect image that I had running around in my head and transferring it to paper as I described it to her. I suppose it was easy for her as sometimes I do have the brain of a ten year old. Always a delight to work with. A great learning experience for her as well, as she skillfully learned how to negotiate various contract proposals for payment of her illustrations. She drives a hard bargain by the way.

Marci Hutchinson, for planting that seed so many years ago. I can still see that hand propped on her hip, head cocked to the side and hear that southern accent of hers say, "Girl, I'm telling you, you need to write a book, I would buy it." "Get your wallet out Marci, I've got twenty copies reserved, just for you."

To each and everyone of you who unknowingly encouraged me by random remarks such as :

I love to read about Pickles
What a great story

When are you going to write a book

Each and every comment was an affirmation that I was truly following the path that God placed before me.

May God bless each of you in return.

Philippians 1:3

I thank my God upon every remembrance of you.

Pickles

A small beagle that has taught me patience and wisdom, as well as Biblical parallels about my own life. A messenger whose life story can reach those that otherwise may not listen, hear or understand. Pickles is God's beagle.

Parable

A simple story used to illustrate a moral or spiritual lesson.

Mark 4:2
Then He (Jesus) taught them many things by parables, and said to them in His teaching...

Mark 12:1
Then he (Jesus) began to speak to them in parables...

Matthew 13:34-35
34 All these things Jesus spoke to the multitude in parables; and without a parable He did not speak to them, 35 that it might be fulfilled which was spoken by the prophet, saying: "I will open My mouth in parables; I will utter things kept secret from the foundation of the world."

Mark 3:23
So He called them to Himself and said to them in parables:

Matthew 13:13
Therefore I speak to them in parables, because seeing they do not see, and hearing they do not hear, nor do they understand.

Chapters

Psalms 119:105
Your word is a lamp to my feet and a light to my path

Pickles' Parables

Genesis 1:25
And God made the beast of the earth according to its kind, cattle according to its kind and everything that creeps on the earth according to its kind. And God saw that it was good.

What is a Beagle

I was blessed to grow up on a farm and was also fortunate to be able to raise beagle pups, both of which I failed to fully appreciate until many years later. The beagle-hood part of my childhood is where this story all begins, so sit back, relax, and enjoy the journey with me.

Simply stated, a beagle is a small breed of dog used primarily to hunt rabbits, and, while being adorably cute to look at, cannot be counted on to stick around and hang out with you. There were plenty of neighborhood kids to keep me entertained as I grew up, so a beagle's company was not necessarily first and foremost in my mind, which was a good thing.

The difference in owning a beagle as a child and owning a beagle as an adult is as different as night and day. As a child, I wasn't held accountable when the beagle hung out in our neighbor's yard all hours of the night howling at the moon. Nor did I have to take all the phone calls that begin with statements such as, "Your dog is on my porch again," your dog jumped on me," "your dog is in my car and won't get out," and so forth and so on. Once I became an adult beagle owner, these problems suddenly became my responsibility.

When I finally decided to get serious about the Pickles' Parables Project, I did a little BFC (beagle fact checking) and was concerned, as well as amused,by some of the facts I found. Of course, at this point it was too late to change anything as Pickles had already established dominance over the entire Brownstead, as well as declaring ownership of everything and everyone within a two mile radius. The entire neighborhood is still trying to figure out how one small beagle now seems to have authority over the whole area. It's as if he is holding all of us hostage.

I have consolidated a few of the more interesting facts from my beagle research project. Most of the information I am sharing is for your protection (in case you are actually thinking of getting a beagle) and for your amusement. The majority of Internet websites I looked at utilized five star rating systems for various dog traits. I have listed a few of the more important ones.

Kid and Family Friendly *****
 • *However, fails to distinguish between family and would-be burglars*

Easy to train   *
 • *Trainable, just independent and stubborn*

Intelligence   ****
 • *I think perhaps manipulative would be a better term*

Wanderlust   *****
 • *More likely fails to pay attention to where they are going.*

Beagles are also noted to have incredible noses which short circuit and control their brains. Thus, the nose is the brain of a beagle in my opinion. While a human has five million scent receptors in their nose, a beagle has 220 million scent receptors in their little snout.

A true beagle will have white in their tail. It may only be a few hairs, but more typically the tip is white. A beagle's owner will also have white in their hair although it may not have been present prior to owning a beagle or perhaps more aptly stated, being owned by a beagle. Last, but not least, is my all-time favorite - in French, "beagle" means loudmouth. The term beagle is thought to have come from the mid-French "bee guele" or, literally, wide throat but more poetically translated as loudmouth. In all fairness to Pickles he is the quietest beagle I have been around. Pickles pretty much limits his barking to rabbit chasing. However, Pickles is sneaky quiet, which in my opinion is as bad or perhaps even worse than barking. I do not like a beagle sneaking up from behind me to pounce on and surprise me or to suddenly appear from out of nowhere at my side.

Those charming little beagle faces are so hard to resist when they look up at you with those innocent little beagle eyes and cock their head. Even as they grow up and gain his or her newfound independence, they still look at you and cock that little head to the side and you are suckered in. It happens to all of us, even with the best intentions. So there you have it, everything you didn't know but that you really needed to know about a beagle.

In summary, a beagle is a happy, intelligent companion that is too busy wandering the neighborhood to be trained. You have to decide what is most important to you at this point. Are you looking for a dog that is dependable, but surly and grumpy, or a dog that appears happy and cheerful on those rare occasions that he is actually home and lying at your feet?

Pickles and Emily

We all get them, the phone calls from scammers and telemarketers, annoying at best but seemingly a fact of life. If that isn't enough, I am now getting phone calls for Pickles. Seriously, I am averaging 4-8 calls a week for him with questions like, "Can Pickles come over?", "Is Pickles home?", or "Does Pickles like Pringles or Lays chips best?". It appears that all the little girls in the neighborhood think Pickles is the best thing since sliced bread.

A few days back a member of his adoring fan club called wanting to know if Pickles could come up for a short visit. To be honest, I was tired and didn't want to go out (especially with Pickles), but this particular young lady has had some struggles in life and usually after about 3 minutes interacting with Pickles she is happy. I decided that I could spare a few minutes of my time to take Pickles for a visit. I hollered for Pickles, "Let's go see Emily!" and immediately he came running, tail wagging, bouncing up and down with ears flopping as he beat me to the car.

It is just a short one mile drive to Emily's house. If it had been a longer drive I would have tied Pickles in the back seat. As it was he was back-seat driving from the front seat, which I find very distracting and annoying. Pickles went from his side to my side, trying his best to grip the steering wheel with his grubby little paws. He leaned on the dash barking directions, or perhaps he was barking at the neighbor's cows. It's hard to tell his barks apart as he uses the same bark for everything and everybody.

When we arrived at Emily's house, I put Pickles' leash on just to be on the safe side, as he is easily distracted by all the deer that frequent her yard. Pickles and I got out of the car, and to be honest I could not tell who was more excited, Pickles or Emily. There was jumping up and down, ears flapping, squeals, waggings, and more, with Pickles imitating Emily's every move in his own beagle style. Pickles was on Emily and Emily was on Pickles. It was a sight to behold...Pure joy on the face of a child and beagle. So engrossed in one another that each was oblivious to the world around them. As predicted, it was three minutes of Pickles licking Emily and in return Pickles being petted and scratched on his belly and behind the ears, at which point Emily was satisfied. It was an intense three minutes that spoke of the love and admiration they have for one another.

Driving home I was reminded of a Bible verse in Matthew. One that I was now able to fully comprehend and understand. Grasping the whole depth of it's meaning. Observing the interaction between Pickles and Emily had made the verse suddenly come alive.

Later that evening Pickles and I sat down and I read to him the verse that had crossed my mind earlier.

Matthew 25:40
Assuredly, I say to you, inasmuch as you did it to one of the least of these my brethren, you did it to Me.

I told Pickles I was proud of him for his enthusiasm in going to see Emily. He had made a young girl's day a little brighter and happier. While I had done nothing more than drive Pickles to Emily's house, I had received so much in return while watching all the energy and fun shared between the two of them. I certainly was blessed more than I deserved. I know in my own spiritual life I give so little, but the smallest act of giving returns to me so much more than I give. I simply can't out give God. Each and every small act is returned to me in ways I simply cannot comprehend. Give without expecting anything in return, then step back and watch what God does.

Deuteronomy 16:17
Every man shall give as he is able, according to the blessing of the Lord your God which He has given you.

Armadillo

It was a bright sunny morning, with the slightest hint of spring in the air. Cool yet crisp without the bone-chilling cold I had grown accustomed to, a nearly perfect March Missouri morning. Grabbing a light jacket, I decided to try and locate Pickles so he could tag along to wear off some of his excess energy, as well as provide some company (for what that would be worth). Stepping out the door, my attention was instantly drawn to the far side of the yard where I spotted Pickles happily hanging out with an armadillo. I don't know why I was surprised by this. He has never exhibited any morals, manners, or good judgment in the past. I quietly stepped back in the house so as not to disturb either of them, and to allow myself to regain composure while observing the two of them. I knew that I would need to develop a strategic plan to deal with this latest episode. A delicate situation to say the least.

Pickles was totally engrossed in the armadillo's various methods of digging, and it appeared, from my standpoint anyway, that Pickles was getting pointers from the armadillo. So, as it was, the armadillo would dig up a small area of yard and then amble a few steps over to start digging up a new area. Pickles would immediately step in where the armadillo had been digging and try to duplicate the same pattern,creating evenly spaced trenches that the lawn mower would clear on one side with a wheel running smack dab down the middle of the trench on the other side. This in turn would cause the lawn mower to be tilted at a 45 degree angle, with a 1/4 of the blade digging in the dirt with the remaining portion of the blade slashing through empty air. This is the sort of thing that drives

Mr. Brown crazy and I needed to put a stop to it immediately. The warm sunshine seemed to spur both of them to a new level of intense hole-digging that I feared would be detrimental to the landscape. Perhaps they may actually dig through the pond bank, resulting in the dam bursting, sending fish all over the yard, and flooding the house, if not sweeping it away. These are the sort of things I have to consider every time Pickles is doing something potentially harmful to not only himself, but the family or the environment. Actually, these are the kind of things I have to consider every time Pickles is out of my sight.

As luck would have it, they suddenly stopped digging, exchanged a few pleasantries, and parted ways. Unnerved by the fact that the discussion amongst them may have in fact been a promise to meet the following day at the same time, I realized I had to put a stop to their relationship in it's present form. In an effort to clear my mind, I went back out for a brisk walk. I was accompanied by Pickles whose breathing was labored and raspy, which I am sure could have been attributed to the dirt that was packed up his nostrils from the big excavation project he had been working on earlier.

Subsequently, I decided to wait until later in the evening to discuss the armadillo situation with Pickles. It was much too nice of a day for unsavory situations.

As evening fell, I sat Pickles down for a little chat about the company he was keeping. I carefully explained that armadillos, while not mean, do have traits that we don't approve of and actions that are not going to be allowed here at the Brownstead, mainly digging up the yard. I went on to explain that when you hang out with people that don't have your same beliefs and standards you sometimes have a tendency to follow along. Of course I know Pickles may not intend to follow along, but Pickles is prone to following the crowd, especially if it appears fun at the time.

I sat Pickles down and we read from the Bible.

First Corinthians 15:33
Do not be deceived: "Evil company corrupts good habits."

Now I am not going to call his little armadillo buddy "bad", however, the armadillo does do some things we consider unacceptable and that upset Mr. Brown. The armadillo digs holes about every six inches with depths ranging from one to eight inches. His inconsistency in depth causes Mr. Brown to become a little unhinged.

Wanting to make sure that Pickles understood what I was trying to tell him, I also read a passage from 2nd Corinthians.

2 Corinthians 6:14
Do not be unequally yoked together with unbelievers. For what fellowship has righteousness with lawlessness? And what communion has light with darkness?

It was at this point that I cautioned Pickles about

hanging around with the armadillo for any extended lengths of time. I also advised Pickles to remove himself from the armadillo's presence when the armadillo begins digging and doing other undesirable things. I did not think it necessary to forbid Pickles from exchanging small talk and such with the armadillo, but advised Pickles against hanging out with the armadillo everyday and becoming best friends.

I have found in my own life that it is so easy for me to pick up on bad habits, and difficult to stay on a righteous path. I certainly am not suggesting that I am better than anyone else, quite the opposite in fact. I am weak and easily influenced. A fact that I am aware of and that satan is also aware of. As a result satan is poised to pounce the millisecond I waiver or question myself in any given situation. satan is ready to help me justify my actions, assuring me that one time won't matter, and hey, everyone else is doing it. Soon one little pebble thrown in the pond creates a ripple effect that is far-reaching. I am not suggesting that I need to isolate myself, but in today's world I have to be very cautious and discerning. I need to be selective and weed out those activities that may be questionable or lead me astray. I need to remain strong and be a light in the darkness around me. If I have doubts or concerns, then it is important that I turn to the Bible. God's word is clear on what is and isn't acceptable behavior. Just because the majority of the population may be participating in something does not make it right. I have found that it is easy to become desensitized and no longer feel any conviction, accepting the wrong as the norm. My best bet is to always see how it lines up with the Bible. Don't rely on your own judgment or what society may tell you is okay. God is the final authority. Ruler over all - past, present, and future.

Isaiah 40:8
The grass withers, the flower fades, But the word of our God stands forever.

Bubble Baths and Beagles

Mr. Brown has always been good at helping out around the house with the exception of washing dishes and beagle baths. In all fairness to Mr. Brown, he placed strong emphasis on the non-dish washing numerous times throughout our courtship, nearly requiring me to sign a release form before he would propose. Of course, neither Mr. Brown nor I knew anything about beagle baths until Pickles came along, at which point it was too late, as well as evident, that beagle baths would be another one of those detestable, but necessary chores. Beagle baths are no doubt a tribulation passed on to me.

As it happened, Mr. Brown and I were sitting out in the yard enjoying one of those picture-perfect summer evenings without a care in the world. The occasional sweet fragrance of mimosas in full bloom wafting gently past on a whisper of a breeze added to the beauty of the moment. Suddenly, without warning, and from out of nowhere we observed a vaporous cloud moving slowly across the yard towards us. As the cloud drew closer, Pickles stepped out at the same time the stench struck Mr. Brown and I with the force of a tsunami. As the offending odor rolled over us, it knocked our senses into overdrive, causing our nostrils to spontaneously clamp shut to prevent further inhalation and potential lung damage. Mr. Brown and I clung to our chairs trying hard to regain our balance and process what was happening.

It was a toxic tragedy unfolding before our eyes. Pickles himself had bloodshot and watery eyes, and it was the first time I have ever observed a dog trying to roll the smell off of themselves. Immediately Mr. Brown gasped,

"Go run some bathwater!", to which I choked back, "I don't want to get near him and fight the bath battle!". Mr. Brown swiftly responded, "Get the water ready and I'll help." Mr. Brown had deemed this an emergency and was prepared to be part of the hazmat team, so I was quick to respond gathering up all the essential cleaning gear.

I quickly filled a metal wash tub with lukewarm water while Mr. Brown rolled up his shirt sleeves and stepped aside to get some fresh air in his lungs.

Knowing that Pickles utterly detests getting a bath, Mr. Brown and I were already prepared with a couple of ropes to tie through his collar to make a cross-tie. Mr. Brown was on one side holding an end of rope, a concrete block was on the other side holding a second rope, Pickles was in the middle of the tub, and I was front and center. As a rule, bathing Pickles quite often develops into a knock-down, man against beast battle, with no real winner, just two survivors. Today, however, was different, with his eyes still burning and red, Pickles was ready to get cleaned up and actually got into his bath water by himself.

After getting Pickles all scrubbed up and smelling somewhat better, I dried him off, and sent him inside while I went back outside to attend to the caustic bath water. Upon arriving back at the water tub, I noticed that the water appeared to be rather murky and slimy, with moans and groans being emitted from the tub. I wasn't certain at this point if it was the wash tub or the water doing all the moaning and groaning. I knew that the toxic sludge had to be moved away from the house and disposed of, and the quicker the better. Dragging the tub away from the house, being ever so careful to not spill a drop of the tainted water on either the ground or myself, I cautiously made my way off the back hillside. Once I had gotten downwind of the house and away from anything that might be harmed by the toxic water, I proceeded to dump it out, being ever so careful as to not splash any on myself. All the surrounding vegetation immediately began wilting from the polluted substance, but as I was also beginning to wither away I didn't feel that there was anything further I could do. Mr. Brown had already collapsed onto the couch, while Pickles had gone straight to bed. We just prayed that the EPA did not conduct a fly-over environmental check.

It was quite some time before we had all settled down, and our nostrils had relaxed enough so that the three of us were finally able to take in sufficient oxygen to regain our sense of balance, as well as gain a little more clarity of mind.

Having survived that nasty little ordeal, I went straight to the shower. What a welcome relief to feel warm, clean water running across my body, while praying the drain didn't clog. Once I felt that I was sufficiently clean I gathered up Pickles and we sat down to read from the Bible.

Isaiah 1:18

"Come now, and let us reason together," says the Lord, "Though your sins are like scarlet, they shall be as white as snow; though they are red like crimson, they shall be as wool."

I explained to Pickles that I did not want to wash his filth off and I detested the task, but Mr. Brown and I did not have a choice. He had to get cleaned up in order to be in the house with us. His filth and smell, if allowed to remain on him, would soon be on us as well as the furniture. We could not and would not allow the stench to be spread throughout the house and intensified.

How glad I am that God wants to clean us up from all our filth and sin...Not because He has to, like we did Pickles, but because He loves us and wants to. God's desire is to see each and every one of us washed white as snow. Jesus paid the "clean up price" when He freely gave His life as atonement for my sin. I can never clean myself up enough to be worthy of God's gift of grace. I am to come with all my filth and baggage, with a humble, believing heart and let God do the cleanup. Only through Jesus' death and resurrection can I ever be clean enough. God will freely forgive and wash everyone clean that seeks Him. God loves to clean us up, not just a spit shine but an inside-and-out, whiter-than-snow wash job.

John 10:10

The thief does not come except to steal, and to kill, and to destroy. I have come that they may have life, and that they may have it more abundantly.

Beagle Bandit

While cooking breakfast recently, I happened to glance out the kitchen window to see Pickles carrying something unfamiliar but moderately large (for a beagle anyway) across the yard. Of course, I could easily write a chapter in a book about the odd variety of unclaimed items Pickles has drug in. Mr. Brown and I do on occasion get concerned about where all this stuff is coming from...is he going to Salvation Army, Goodwill, the local dump or worse yet the neighbor's front porch? After breakfast I decided that I better go find out what Pickles had now decorated the front porch with. "For Sale", he has a "for sale" sign, not only that but he is very calmly sitting by it, as if he were in fact "for sale". I am a little bit offended that he doesn't appreciate the hand that pours out the "Beagle Bits" to him every morning and night whether he's been good or bad. Pickles is becoming quite the ungrateful little pooch. I might just change that sign to "For Free". I picked Pickles up (with all his ill - gotten goods) and we went to read from the Bible.

1 Timothy 6:7-8
7 For we brought nothing into this world, and it is certain we can carry nothing out.
8 And having food and clothing, with these we shall be content.

At this point I am uncertain if Pickles feels he needs these items, or if he gets a beagle thrill from dragging all these "treasures" in. Of course, as a parent I would like to think, "Is he just trying to bring me gifts to make me happy?"

It didn't end there. As soon as we moved into mowing season, the stealing seemed to escalate for a short time before finally tapering off, but not before it had caused Mr. Brown great anguish as he attempted to mow around all the clutter haphazardly strewn throughout the Brownstead. Mr. Brown is an amazing man. He works hard all day, and during the mowing months (March thru October) he comes home and metamorphosizes into a "lean, mean mowing machine" the ultimate "lawn ranger".

Mr. Brown takes great pride in his yard, and it is reflected by the park like beauty that he works hard to maintain. We did, at one time, have a magazine cover type yard, peaceful, tranquil, and beautiful...until Pickles arrived on the scene and we had a hostile beagle take over. My first thought was that Pickles was a pack rat. Any time we were out of sight for two minutes or more he would find sticks, stones, bones, paper, plastic, vegetables, road signs, furniture, and other unidentifiable objects and lay them out in an unorganized manner all over the yard. With time, I have come to suspect we have a far more serious problem going on, that perhaps Pickles is a kleptomaniac. I did not jump to this conclusion lightly, as no one wants to believe that their beagle has a problem. However, when a man's belt showed up, followed by a large piece of foam, a stuffed rabbit, a deer hunter orange hat, a frisbee, and then a flower pot (how on earth did he get a large flower pot hauled in here?), I became suspicious.

Ephesians 4:28
Let him who stole steal no longer, but rather let him labor, working with his hands what is good, that he may have something to give him who has need.

I started to think about stealing and why would anyone take something that doesn't belong to them. I then thought about the various ways of stealing, and how probably all of us have been guilty at one time or the other. Did you bring home a pen, note pad, stamp or anything from your job that you did not pay for? Sad to say, but I plead guilty to the following..."stealing time." Yes, my coffee break went 18 minutes, instead of the 15 minutes we were allowed. It seems innocent, 3 minutes, but when it becomes the norm, that can add up to quite a bit in a year. 3 minutes X 5 days =15 minutes a week. Add it up and you come up with 13 hours a year. Far worse is when I get too busy to read God's word and use that time for something else. I am stealing from my relationship with Christ. I am embarrassed by what a thief I am. The Bible is plain that no man is just or good, we all have messed up, but God's grace is quick to forgive if we are repentant.

Ecclesiastes 7:20
For there is not a just man on earth who does good and does not sin.

Romans 3:10
As it is written: "There is none righteous, no, not one"

Ephesians 2:8-9

8 For by grace you have been saved through faith, and that not of yourselves; it is the gift of God. 9 not of works, lest anyone should boast.

How grateful I am for grace. Without God's grace I would not have a chance in this life. Grace freely given with no strings attached. Dear Lord, I pray that I may also extend grace to those who are in need, expecting nothing in return.

Psalms 141:3
Set a guard, O Lord, over my mouth; Keep
watch over the door of my lips.

Beetle Bugs and Beagle Lips

It was a welcome relief to wake up to a cooler morning after a long, hot, dry spell. The grass had been washed clean by an unexpected but welcome rain during the night, and the air was heavy with the intoxicating scent of fresh, damp earth. It was the perfect morning to walk across the yard while sipping that second cup of coffee. Pickles had already disappeared outside to do whatever it is he does (that I don't want to know about), so I was in hopes of a peaceful morning without him underfoot.

I made it across the yard to my garden area before I noticed Pickles sprawled on the lawn, chewing on his lips. Had Pickles been napping or looking around, I would not have given him a second look, but it was the chewing and rolling of his mouth and lips as if he had a huge wad of chewing tobacco that caught my attention. With his history of getting into things, it could very well have been chewing tobacco, and so I felt it was best to find out what he had going on in his mouth. Of course, being the beagle that he is, he decided to lead me on a slow chase across the yard, all while he is still chewing, rolling his lips, and spitting. I can assure you that rolling, spitting beagle lips are not a pretty sight. After a few moments of this game of his, he decided to lay down while continuing his chewing, spitting, and lip rolling. I carefully pried opened his mouth (just in case there was tobacco juice in there) and immediately saw one of those Japanese beetles (the shiny, hard-shelled ones that had recently devoured every peach off my tree) nonchalantly walking around Pickles' gum line, across the roof of his mouth, and back across his tongue like it was an every day excursion for the beetle. I managed to get the beetle out of his mouth, and immediately, Pickles was nipping at the beetle again. One would think that by now he had learned a lesson, but apparently he had not. Countless times I've watched Pickles jump and snap at whatever bug/object flies by him, his eyes growing large when he has made a catch, then gagging and swallowing quickly. I just shake my head and say, "Pickles, sometimes you don't have the sense that God gave a goose." Then suddenly it occurs to me that Pickles goes to bed when he wants, gets up when he wants, and is hand fed gourmet beagle bits whenever he wants. Maybe, just maybe.........he is smarter than me?

I explained to Pickles that we all make mistakes, often because we do not know better. To continue doing the same thing (snapping at every bug) after having knowledge of the outcome is going to produce the same unwanted results and get him (or us) in trouble. It is only a matter of time until he snaps at a wasp and, with his luck, catches it. I casually mentioned that perhaps he should lay off the bug- snapping habit. If he sees a bug, he should turn and walk the other way to avoid any further temptation.

We sat down later and I read to him from the Bible.

Proverbs 22:3
A prudent man foresees evil and hides himself, but the simple pass on and are punished.

Proverbs 19:20
Listen to counsel and receive instruction, that you may
be wise in your latter days.

I thought of my own life and the things that I knew
were not healthy for my Christian walk, but my sinful
nature kept pulling me towards them. It is at that
moment, I need to get down to some serious praying, turn
away, and listen to wise counsel. God does not want to see
his children hurt, but sometimes we insist on doing what we
shouldn't, and we have to swallow a few bugs in order to
learn. Not a pleasant experience for sure, but oftentimes
necessary. I've swallowed more bugs than I care to admit
to, but God, with mercy and grace, has always been quick to
exterminate my bugs when I humbly come to Him with a
repentive heart.

Big and Hairy

A couple weeks back, Mr. Brown and I were sitting out on the balcony relaxing while enjoying a homemade root beer. It was one of those perfect nights with enough moonlight to allow us to have some vision of things below us...mainly Pickles. It wasn't long before Pickles came strolling in from wherever it is that beagles tend to hang out and do whatever it is that they do. As is customary, Pickles was zig-zagging from one corner of the yard to the other, while taking note of all the different smells that his keen little nose was detecting. Suddenly, the brakes went on, the hair and tail stiffened, and he came to a stop. Clearly he had spotted something we could not see from our vantage point.

Pickles commenced to bouncing forward with a little bark and then leaping rapidly backwards all while barking, growling, and nipping. After a minute or two of observing his behavior, Mr. Brown turned to me and said, "You better go see what he's got cornered, it could be a snake." I love how Mr. Brown so easily suggested that I be the one to go check the situation out. I, being the submissive wife that I am however, made my way down the stairs and outside to see what all the commotion was about. Just to be on the safe side, I slipped on my snake-stomping rubber boots that I keep conveniently located by the front door. I cautiously approached the situation and finally was able to make out a small squatty toad! "Good grief Pickles! It's a toad for crying out loud! Stop acting like a puppy." I finally got him settled down, assuring him that the toad would not be a detriment to our safety, and we then made our way into the house. We talked about getting all excited over something so small and letting fear take control.

I saw this as a good opportunity to tell Pickles about the time something similar happened to me and how I also may have over-reacted.

It happened several years back while our daughters were still living at home. I had moseyed into our bathroom and had just got all situated to rid myself of the pot of coffee I had drank a few moments earlier, when there arose a horrible disturbance in one corner of the bathroom. As it so happened, there was a bottle of bleach sitting there which appeared to be quivering and violently shaking. From my vantage point I could not positively identify what was behind the bottle and in the room with me, but my imagination made several quick assumptions, none of which were pleasant, and probably not accurate either. It was at this point that I did what any self-respecting person about to be attacked would do, I ran from the bathroom yelling, "It's big and it's hairy!!!". Now this got Mr. Brown's attention pretty quickly and he was immediately up ready to defend his family. Somewhere between the 4.7 seconds of my departure from the life-threatening situation and Mr. Brown's arrival on the scene, the "big and hairy" had escaped and a small toad was left in its place. I still to this day don't know how the "big and hairy" made it out of the bathroom unnoticed by the rest of the family. Another one of life's unsolved mysteries. It took several weeks for the family to recover and get over the fear of something big and hairy attacking and eating us in the middle of the night. Time heals and puts to rest all things and this was no different.

After I had told Pickles about my "big and hairy", he and I talked about letting something small scare us until we cannot think rationally and the small keeps getting bigger and bigger, until we become defeated and lose all hope. I got the Bible out, and Pickles and I read some scripture verses.

Joshua 1:9

Have I not commanded you? Be strong and of good courage; do not be afraid, nor be dismayed, for the Lord your God is with you wherever you go

Psalms 56: 3-4

3 Whenever I am afraid, I will trust in You. 4 In God (I will praise His word),
In God I have put my trust; I will not fear. What can flesh do to me?

Romans 8:38-39

38 For I am persuaded that neither death nor life, nor angels nor principalities nor powers, nor things present nor things to come,
39 nor height nor depth, nor any other created thing, shall be able to separate us from the love of God which is in Christ Jesus our Lord.

To live in fear is to put my faith and trust in earthly things and not rely on God. It is all too easy to become fearful, it happens to me quite frequently. satan wants me to be afraid and live in fear, then he has control over me. satan is a master of deceit making innocent things appear to be fearsome. For me to allow fear to overtake my life is to deny God's power and love.

It is during fearful moments that I need to slow down, take a deep breath, and remind myself that God didn't say He might take care of me. God declared His limitless love for me by giving His Son to die for my sins. If He loves me that much, He will most assuredly take care of me.

Revelation 21:4

And God will wipe away every tear from their eyes; there shall be no more death, nor sorrow, nor crying. There shall be no more pain, for the former things have passed away.

Broken Ribs

The morning began like so many of our other Sunday mornings with Mr. Brown and I enjoying a steaming cup of coffee on the balcony before getting ready for church. As is our custom, we were watching Pickles in the yard below as he was getting geared up to leave the premises. Pickles was casually strolling the premises when he made a sudden abrupt turn and began dog-trotting up and out our driveway. I yelled down to him, "Pickles get back here!" He responded in his usual manner by continuing on his journey. I have determined over the course of time that he has a somewhat predictable route that he follows, leaving me with some idea of where he may be lurking, and what innocent individuals are being harassed at any given time. Not 100% accurate but near enough that I can work with and narrow down his location to about any given county. This has proven beneficial when it is getting dark and Pickles has not returned home yet. I do not want late night phone calls from irritated neighbors, and I do all in my power to prevent this from happening.

As Mr. Brown and I traveled home from church that day, we slowed down as we drove by one of Pickles' favorite hangouts, so that he would know that we were heading home. Neither Mr. Brown or I saw him, so it was anybody's guess at that point as to Pickles' exact whereabouts.

Wonder of wanders (pun intended), when we got home, Pickles was actually on the front porch waiting.
At this point, Pickles typically blasts over to the car and jumps in before we can get out, causing quite a disturbance as we try to untangle him from our laps. Pickles did none

of that on this particular day. Mr. Brown got to the porch before I did and turns quickly to me, "Pickles can't move his back legs." Of course, this gets my adrenaline pumping, and I arrive on the scene in record time, having been catapulted by the adrenaline rush from one side of the car to the other. It is obvious that something is seriously wrong. Pickles right hip was significantly swollen, he was shaking, drooling, and was glassy eyed. My first inclination was that he had been bit by a snake as they are very common in our area during this time of year and his symptoms were typical of a snake bite.

There was no question that I would be taking Pickles for medical treatment, on a Sunday (double your money) no doubt. After a quick, frantic phone call I was put in touch with the on-call veterinarian, Dr. Erica M. Smith, DVM of Animal Health Center in Rolla, MO and with Mr. Brown's help we were able to get Pickles loaded in the car. It was a very nerve racking drive for me, wondering if Pickles would still be alive once I reached the veterinary office, which was a 25 minute drive from our house. Dr. Smith quickly determined that Pickles appeared very tender in his rib cage area. She felt this tenderness was an indication of broken ribs or torn muscles instead of a snake bite. A series of x-rays were taken to determine what, if anything, was broken.

To make a long story short, Pickles had encountered something, perhaps a car, truck, horse, or cow. We will never know for certain. The resulting injury was two cracked ribs and one small bulging disc in his spine. He was a mess, and I was mess. Together, we appeared (me more

than Pickles) to be a big bundle of quivering nerves.
However, God is always one to provide reassurance if we
just open our eyes and look, fully expecting. While waiting
for Dr. Smith to determine the extent of Pickles injuries,
I happened to notice the title of the book that she had
carried in and laid down. While she continued to examine
and work with Pickles, I picked up the book and read a
chapter from "*Heaven hears each whisper-answered
prayers in everyday life.*" There was no doubt in my mind
that this was divine intervention and encouragement as well
as words of comfort for me during a very anxious time. It
was God's way of reassuring me that He is in control of my
life as well as the life of one small beagle. Neither man nor
animal are insignificant to God, for all are His creations.
We were going to be okay.

Pickles was able to come home, heavily sedated. I got to
wait on him hand and foot while trying to coax
him into eating. Pickles is still a brat, but since I like him a
little bit my heart ached for him and the pain he
was suffering. A pain he had to endure until his cracked
ribs were healed. A direct result of disobedience.
I read to Pickles later that evening, although he was
groggy, and I don't think it sank in much.

Psalms 147:3
He heals the brokenhearted and binds up their wounds.

That verse covered us both, my broken heart for the
suffering he was going through, and Pickles' for his
physical wounds. God will heal and bind both, spiritual and
physical breaks.

I felt like Pickles needed a little encouragement, but I also wanted to remind him that he had been disobedient, and, as a result, was suffering the consequences. In addition, he brought pain to me as well...not to mention that my bank account was crying the blues.

I could not immediately fix the broken ribs; Pickles had to suffer for quite some time, as the healing process was slow. This was a direct result of doing what he wanted and being disobedient. Per Dr. Smith's orders, Pickles also lost 4 weeks of any running around privileges, to provide the necessary time for his ribs to heal properly. Those were direct consequences of poor,selfish decisions. As children of God, aren't we much the same way? We go against God's will in our lives and get hurt (physically or spiritually), and come dragging back wanting a quick fix. God is quick to forgive, but sometimes the self-inflicted pain takes awhile to heal.

God's heart breaks for us. God doesn't want to see us suffer, that is why He gave us guidelines for living. I know that I am stubborn and want to do my own thing, and, as a result, I suffer a lot of pain and grief that could have been avoided, oftentimes causing others pain and hurt in the process. God knows best and has promised to help us when temptation comes, and temptation will come.

1 Corinthians 10:13

No temptation has overtaken you except such as is common to man; but God is faithful, who will not allow you to be tempted beyond what you are able, but with the temptation will also make the way of escape, that you may be able to bear it.

Psalms 127:3
Behold, children are a heritage from the Lord, The fruit of the womb is a reward.

Pickles and the Chainsaw

by guest author
Cash B. Calhoun

During a recent visit with our daughter and the little people, I was asked for another story about Pickles' latest adventures. Always anticipating their request, I try to keep in mind what his latest escapade has been. Of course, Pickles is always up to something, so I never seem to have a shortage of Pickles' Tails (pun intended). It was after I had finished telling them the latest episode that our oldest grandson Cash (8 at the time) disappeared.....

Pickles and the Chainsaw

Once upon a time, Pickles was taking a hike. He found a junkyard, and he saw a chainsaw. He went inside and looked at the chainsaw for a couple of minutes. He grabbed it with his paws and saw a button. He took it to a tree and pushed the button. Then do you know what he did? He cut the tree down, he pushed the button again and the chainsaw turned off. Somebody saw him, and paid him money because that tree needed cut down.

He took the money, and then he sawed the house down. The person chased him. When the person left, Pickles built a better house with his tools, then Pickles ran off. The person came back and was excited. He told Granny B what a good dog Pickles was. The end.

I then asked Cash what Bible verse he thought should go with the story and in his own words.

Romans 8:28
And we know that all things work together for good to those who love God, to those who are called according to His purpose.

What a great reminder from a child that God can take the worst situation and spin it 180 degrees into something good. Taking the bad and turning it into a blessing. A blessing bigger and better than we could ever have dreamed up.

We must hold fast to our faith even when things look dim, and our world seems to be falling down around us. God will build back, bigger and better. If you don't believe me then read the book of Job. Talk about a guy that had it all, lost it all, and regained more than he lost. Job was a man who feared God and shunned evil. A gem in God's eyes. God blessed Job with 7 sons, 3 daughters, 7000 sheep, 3000 camels, 500 yoke of oxen, 500 female donkeys and a very large household. I would venture to say that Job had numerous servants, shepherds, farm hands and the best coffee money could buy. Job also would have owned a large parcel of property. Job had faith in God and God also had faith in Job, trusting that Job would remain true to his beliefs. As it was, satan came along to stir up some trouble and as a result Job lost everything, and I do mean everything. Job lost all his livestock, his sons, and daughters, but in his most distraught and tormented state, he did not deny God. Job did in fact curse the day he was born (who wouldn't?), but still maintained his faithfulness to God.

Job 1 21-22

21 And he said: "Naked I came from my mother's womb, and naked shall I return there. The Lord gave and the Lord has taken away; Blessed be the name of the Lord." 22 In all this Job did not sin nor charge God with wrong.

At this point I would have been a little more than discouraged and upset. I would have been crying a river of tears while sobbing, "Why me? Why me?"

This guy (Job) was blameless. However, Job loved God, and despite all the tragedy his faith in God remained steadfast, even after Job's wife told him, "Curse God." How's that for marital support? Job lost all his worldly possessions, animals, and children but not his faith. As a result, God blessed him with twice as much as he previously had. Evidence that God does in fact take the bad (or horrible in this case) and create a new and good thing if our faith remains steadfast in Him.

Cats and Toys

A few mornings back, I happened to glance out the window only to notice a rather large, ugly alley cat strolling around the driveway. I nonchalantly mentioned it to Pickles, who, at that point, seemed totally disinterested. I then casually said, "Well how about that? That ole tom cat is playing with your toys Pickles." Pickles' disinterest turned into immediate interest and hysteria as he nearly tore the door off the hinges in an effort to get outside and gather up his treasures. After an ugly-looking confrontation, in which several meows and barks were exchanged, Pickles started gathering up his toys and bringing them into the house. Funny how a few seconds before it was okay to leave his toys out, but let some of his neglected treasures that were scattered around the yard get touched by a cat and it was a whole different attitude. If I could teach him to pick up as quickly and efficiently as he did on that particular morning I could safely walk through the house without tripping over his multitude of sticks, bones, and toys. I don't foresee that happening anytime soon, but one can always hope. I was somewhat concerned that Pickles had suddenly become so selfish and unfriendly, worrying more about his material possessions than the ole tom cat. Not an attitude I wanted to encourage in any way.

I tried to nicely explain (while keeping his self-esteem intact) that fighting a cat was not a good idea. If he didn't get his eyes scratched out, he would probably still wind up with cat scratch fever and that was not a good thing either...not to mention cat hair in his mouth, which I am sure he would find distasteful. Cats also are notorious for carrying grudges indefinitely and, therefore, just because he thought the fight was over, it wasn't over. Cats are sneaky, deceitful, spiteful, and also are vengeful creatures. I advised Pickles to avoid a cat fight, regardless of losing his toys. Some fights you just cannot win.

I also reminded Pickles that he had 85 acres loaded with rabbits to chase, dirt to dig in, ponds to swim in, and a strawberry patch (that he frequents without my permission) loaded with ripe strawberries. Why should he worry about a few cheaply made plastic toys when he has the whole outdoors here, as well as the neighbors' yards and porches?

As I have to do quite frequently, I got the Bible down and read to Pickles from Matthew.

Matthew 6:19-21
19 Do not lay up for yourselves treasures on earth, where moth and rust destroy and where thieves break in and steal;
20 but lay up for yourselves treasures in heaven, where neither moth nor rust destroys and where thieves do not break in and steal.
21 For where your treasure is, there your heart will be also.

I then began to think how I sometimes (more than I like to admit to) worry more about my possessions than people. How sad that must make God feel when I treasure stuff over people. It doesn't matter what I have here on earth, what matters is what I store up in heaven. What I have here will fade away, what I store up in heaven will remain forever.

My focus can very quickly turn to earthly treasures if I am not careful. I look at what other people have and do a comparison check and dwell on what I don't have instead of all the blessings I do have. Real contentment only comes from a personal relationship with Christ. When I take time to focus on Christ, the things of the earth grow dim and less desirable.

Collusion's

Had it not been for Mr. Brown's recollection of an old childhood fable along with all the recent talk on the news of "Russian Collusions", I would still be scratching my head over Pickles' sudden and puzzling behavior.

It began when I noticed the local rabbits were becoming bolder, going so far as to lay around the yard, with seemingly no cares or worries. At any given time, I could walk out the front door and find several rabbit clumps (a rabbit clump contains a minimum of 3 rabbits) lounging in the sun. More often than not, Pickles would stroll right on by, seemingly oblivious to the rabbit clumps. The rabbits, in turn, were no more concerned about a beagle being nearby than they were by a leaf falling from a tree. On rare occasions, Pickles would trot towards a rabbit and give a small, half-hearted beagle bark, which would result in the rabbits moving a couple feet before settling back into their comfort zone. Up until this time, Pickles lived to hunt rabbits, and now suddenly, he was totally unmotivated to give chase. He was content to leave them at peace in the yard. More concerning to me was the fact that a couple of the rabbit clumps had moved their carefree grazing area dangerously near to my garden area. I came to the conclusion that perhaps it was too hot for Pickles to chase rabbits, and I decided not to worry about it for the time being. If his lackadaisical behavior carried over into the winter months, then I would be concerned and take appropriate action to resolve the issue.

It was also near this same time that I stumbled across numerous turtle shells strewn haphazardly around the yard. Had it been only one or two vacant shells, I would not have given it a second thought. As it was, the shells were showing up with a regularity that was somewhat alarming. To be quite honest, the thought of naked turtles wandering around the hillsides was just downright disturbing. At this point in time, however, I still had not connected the brazen bunnies with this sudden turtle shell issue.

After listening to the morning news as they talked about the "Russian Collusion" Mr. Brown suggested the possibility of a rabbit-beagle collusion. Suddenly it made perfect sense. The rabbits are still mad over getting beat by the tortoise in "that race". They have never forgiven the turtle population for the actions of one small, determined turtle. Somehow, someway, the rabbits had managed to "collude" with Pickles and convinced him to take their side. As a result, Pickles took it upon himself to declare war on turtles. I am still trying to sort out how they managed to persuade him, unless a large number of rabbits had created a bunny bully gang, "The Hateful Hares".

For those of you who are not familiar with what you falsely perceive to be cute, fluffy, little bunnies, allow me to enlighten you. Rabbits are mean, it's that plain and simple, they bite and kick. If you don't believe me, go ask anyone who has raised rabbits. Until you have had a rabbit back up to you and lay one across your shin bone with those hind legs you don't know about "bad bunnies".

Several years ago our girls had a pet rabbit, "Carl". They also had a beagle,"Ladybug". Every morning, Ladybug went outside and immediately Carl backed up and kicked

Ladybug across her nose or backside (whichever was most convenient for Carl) sending Ladybug yelping in the other direction. It didn't take Ladybug long to realize it was an inevitable part of her morning routine and something needed to change. Ladybug changed which door she went out of in the morning to avoid Carl at all costs. She continued to chase rabbits outside of the perimeter of the yard but did not even so much as make eye contact with those in the yard. This same thing appears to be happening with Pickles, so I have to assume something similar has happened. In no way did I want Pickles involved in this apparent ongoing feud. An incident from years ago in which there needed to be forgiveness and the "hares needed to hurry along".

I sat Pickles down later that evening and read from the Bible.

Isaiah 5:20

Woe to those who call evil good, and good evil; who put darkness for light, and light for darkness, who put bitter for sweet and sweet for bitter!

I explained to Pickles that he had jumped to collusion conclusions and had never stopped to question whether the turtle had really done anything wrong to the rabbits. The turtle, in fact, had minded his own business keeping his focus on running the race to the best of his abilities. The rabbit, all puffed up with pride and arrogance, didn't feel like he had to keep focused. Rabbits, after all are the fastest by a hundred fold and there was no way a slow-poke turtle was going to beat him. The turtle followed the rules of the race, and although it was nearly impossible for him to win, he in fact won. The hare, on the other hand, was so full of himself that he partied, chewed up a couple prized cabbage plants, threw snide remarks towards the turtle, and forgot all about the race to be run. The resulting hare loss was not the turtle's fault. Pride and arrogance lost the race. I told Pickles he was not to be involved with bitter and unforgiving bunnies. In his failure to question, he (Pickles) had been deceived into thinking that the bad (bunnies) were good and the good (turtle) was bad. It's an easy trap to fall into if one is not discerning and careful. He needed to be on guard at all times, and if he had any doubts, he should seek out someone who knew.

In our own lives, Christ has given us a race to run, with the final prize of dwelling forever with Him in heaven. We need to focus on that race set before us, and continue on at a steady pace. Each one of us will have a different set of stumbling blocks along our race pathway, obstacles that may slow us down, but they should never be used as an excuse to stop. We need to be careful not to feel that we are better than anyone else, or that it's an easy race, so we don't have to try. It is when we begin to think we are better than others that we lose focus and stray off the path. We cannot blame others for our stumbling, we all have the same set of race rules - "The Bible". Don't let someone convince you that you can go against the rules and still win. It won't happen. satan will present good as bad and bad as good, all a lie to distract us from finishing the race.

What a great reminder that we do not have to be the

fastest or the best to complete the race.

We will stumble and fall. Pick yourself up, dust yourself off and keep going. Remembering also, that our fellow racers will at some point fall. It is then we need to be quick to help them up, and encourage them to finish the race. A steady but faithful pace will still get us to the finish line.

I know in my day-to-day life I sometimes face tasks that loom large and seem overwhelming. I picture in my mind the end goal and work a little bit each day towards that goal. Most days I can't see the progress, but then a week later I can step back, look it over, and say, "Wow, I've gotten a lot done. I am closer to my goal." The same is true with our spiritual life. We need to be steady, consistent, and grounded in faith, knowing we will make it. The finish line will be worth the steady pace to get there. Don't let the distance scare ya, just get moving!

Hebrews 12:1-2

1 Therefore we also, since we are surrounded by so great a cloud of witnesses, let us lay aside every weight, and the sin which so easily ensnares us, and let us run with endurance the race that is set before us,

2 looking unto Jesus, the author and finisher of our faith, who for the joy that was set before Him endured the cross, despising the shame, and has sat down at the right hand of the throne of God.

Coon-Hunters

Mr. Brown and I were winding down from a blessed and Merry Christmas, reminiscing about the time we had spent with loved ones and all the laughter that had been shared. As we were fondly recalling the faces of the little people as they excitedly tore open their gifts, we were interrupted by a knock at the door. Pickles immediately was at full attention, arriving at the front door before Mr. Brown or I ever heard the second knock, or had time to process the thought that one of us needed to get up and go see who might be here on Christmas night. Pickles could have been thinking Santa Claus had forgot to leave a gift, or, worse yet, after Santa checked his naughty/nice list, might be repossessing something he had left.

Turns out, it was a neighbor from across the hillside, stopping by to ask permission to go coon-hunting. Pickles was beside himself with excitement and glee until I told him he was not going coon-hunting. As the hunters went on their Merry Christmas coon-hunting way, Pickles proceeded to throw a temper tantrum right smack dab in the middle of the dining room floor. He barked, howled, jumped up and down, ran circles, got the hair on his back all fuzzed up...you name it, Pickles did it, and did it with great zeal. It was not a short tantrum either, he tantrumed on and on and on. Fortunately for me my hearing has diminished by several decibels, and I was able to go to the other room while he continued with his outburst. Continue on he did, for about 15 minutes. At this point, I could tell by the way the hair was starting to stand up on Mr. Brown that he himself was getting a little agitated, and it was time that I intervene. I went to the dining room and retrieved the troubled, fit-throwing beagle, plopped him on my lap (all while he was still kicking and howling), grabbed the Bible, and proceeded to read to him.

1 Peter 4:10
As each one has received a gift, minister it to one another, as good stewards of the manifold grace of God.

Ephesian 2:10
For we are His workmanship, created in Christ Jesus for good works, which God prepared beforehand that we should walk in them.

I explained to Pickles that his gift was the ability to smell rabbits and also to hear them as they tip-toe towards my garden. When he observes a rabbit in close proximity to my garden he is supposed to give them directions to the neighbor's garden (just kidding neighbors).

I struggled to be delicate with Pickles and not hurt his self-esteem but still get my point across.
Not wanting to hurt his feelings, I carefully explained that his size would be a detriment in coon-hunting, as coons, in general, tend to be taller and fatter than Pickles himself. God had created Pickles specifically for rapid rabbit removal, and it would be in his best interest to stick with this God-given purpose.

I then thought of my own life, and that, in my own weakness, I do not always want to use the gifts that God has blessed me with. I see other gifts I would prefer to have and compare myself to others. Once I start up my comparison chart, I find myself a very unhappy and ungrateful person. Almost immediately, satan steps in trying to convince me that my gift is useless and not doing any good, so why not give it up? I have to remind myself that God created me (and you) in a very unique way to carry out His plan. Each one of us is a piece to a larger puzzle that fits perfectly together. A puzzle with even one small piece missing is incomplete. Each puzzle piece has its place to complete the whole picture. We must always remember to be mindful that each gift from God is special and equally important...none being elevated above the other.

Pickles was sullen the rest of the evening, but luckily, by morning time, he seemed to either have slept it off, or forgotten, and was back to his rabbit removal job...doing exactly what God had intended for little beagles to do.

Romans 12:3-8

3 For I say, through the grace given to me, to everyone who is among you, not to think of himself more highly than he ought to think, but to think soberly, as God has dealt to each one a measure of faith.

4 For as we have many members in one body, but all the members do not have the same function,

5 so we, being many, are one body in Christ, and individually members of one another.

6 Having then gifts differing according to the grace that is given to us, let us use them: if prophecy, let us prophesy in proportion to our faith;

7 or ministry, let us use it in our ministering: he who teaches, in teaching: 8 he who exhorts, in exhortation; he who gives; with liberality; he who leads, with diligence; he who shows mercy, with cheerfulness.

Psalms 23:4

Yea, though I walk through the valley of the shadow of death, I will fear no evil; for You are with me; Your rod and Your staff, they comfort me

Cora Bell

1944-2017

Although we live in the country and on a dead-end road, I still like to put Pickles in his large chain-link pen when I leave for work each morning. This prevents phone calls from the neighborhood, and ensures that I do not have to go beagle hunting when I get home from work. There are some mornings in which Pickles makes a sudden disappearance before I get him locked up and some mornings when he is able to convince me he will behave. Mr. Brown and I are trying to prevent Pickles from becoming a nuisance in the neighborhood, although I fear it may, in fact, be too late.

Mr. Brown and I live down a private lane off from the main county road. On those mornings that Pickles leaves the premises, he travels up our driveway crosses the road to a large brick house. I am told that Pickles sits down in their yard and smiles in the window at Cora, the lady that lives there. Pickles then waits patiently for Paul, the man of the house to step outside to say, "Hi" and give Pickles a scratch behind the ears. After a tail wag in return, Pickles strolls over to their barnyard and barks a good morning to Sonny the horse. Sonny drops his head, looks Pickles in the eye, and responds with a horse sigh and soft neigh as they touch noses. Then, it's time to hi-tail it (pun intended) to his next destination, the home of his two very best friends, Noah and Mallory. Noah is a huge, hairy yellow dog and Mallory is an adorable, blond-haired, blue-eyed five year old girl. Noah enjoys the visits, and he and Pickles play some jumping games, tail chewing, rolling on one another, and slobbering on one another to see who can get who the dirtiest. Mallory loves Pickles, and Pickles loves

Mallory. Pickles lets Mallory carry him all over their yard, and Mallory lets Pickles chew on her toys. Everyone is happy, and I, upon returning home, merely slow down and honk as I drive by and Pickles heads home.

The couple that lives directly across the road are Mr. Brown's relatives. Cora is Mr. Brown's aunt, and she has been battling a terminal illness for the past couple of years. Cora always maintained a positive and upbeat attitude, rejoicing and finding happiness in the smallest of things, even a beagle sitting in her yard looking in her window as if to say, "Hi, I hope you are feeling better today." Cora mentioned to me how much she enjoys Pickles' early morning visits to check in on her. For this reason, I have relaxed my control (as if I ever had any... ha!) on his whereabouts and let Pickles have a little more wandering freedom.

As time passed we knew that Cora's time here on earth was drawing to a close and I think somehow Pickles sensed it also. As it always is with our loved ones, the time had come much faster than we wanted. Hospice came in to make sure her final days were the best they could be. Family and friends were stopping by to spend a few moments and share some favorite memories with Cora as well. The family had begun preparing for her passing on to her heavenly home. I began to feel a stirring in my spirit, and, after considerable thought and prayer, I felt that I should take Pickles by to see her. Cora always loved to see Pickles, and although she was unable to play with him, she looked forward to his morning visits.

That, combined with frequents texts from Cora asking how Pickles is doing, telling me how cute he is, and what a good dog he is, helped affirm my decision to take him for a final visit. I was somewhat apprehensive as he can be quite rowdy, but I knew in my heart it was the right thing to do. Making certain I had a tight hold on him, Pickles and I went to see Cora. Immediately we were greeted with, "There's my little buddy come to see me he wants me to get well." Clearly, I had made the right choice. I carried Pickles to her bedside and as Cora reached up to pet Pickles, he gently licked her hand. A bittersweet memory forever etched in my heart.

A soft and solemn dog saying his final goodbye. I kept our visit brief. I was proud of Pickles behavior, and I scratched him behind the ears and told him what a good beagle he had been.

I read to Pickles that evening from Romans, and we discussed how doing the right thing is not always easy, but we have an obligation to do what God calls us to do.

Romans 15:1-2
We then who are strong ought to bear with the scruples of the weak, and not to please ourselves. 2 Let each of us please his neighbor for his good, leading to edification.

It's not easy to see a loved one struggle; it hurts and saddens us. So often I hear people say, "I don't want to see them like that. I want to remember them as they were, so I can't go visit." Romans is pretty clear we have an obligation. It may not be easy, but it's not about us. God's grace will give us the strength we need. I was rewarded with a bittersweet moment in which I was blessed to see Cora smile and hear, "There's my little buddy."

3 John 1:4
I have no greater joy than to hear that my children walk in the truth

Cora passed away four days after Pickles last visit.

Psalms 34:17

The righteous cry out, and the Lord hears,
And delivers them out of all of their
troubles.

Coyotes

Mr. Brown and I are blessed to live out in the country surrounded by wooded areas and soft wide meadows... peaceful and full of solitude (until we brought home Pickles that is). Mr. Brown and I feel safe, comfortable, and at peace here.

There are things native to this area that can inflict pain or present a danger. We are aware of this and know what we need to watch for and avoid. For instance, in the warmer months one is always careful of reaching into, under, or over any object until you are certain wasps have not built a nest. One sting of a mad wasp and you learn quickly to be on the lookout.

Snakes are another concern. Missouri boasts both poisonous and non-poisonous snakes. If a snake is outside, walk far and wide, or don't bother it and it probably will not bother you.

Poison Ivy is a nasty little weed that can cause a bumpy rash that itches like there is no tomorrow. Not everyone is allergic to poison ivy. There are some very fortunate individuals that are spared the intense itchy agony of poison ivy. I am not one of the lucky ones. There is also the wide array of stickers, thistles, briars, and many other sticky, stabby plants whose sole purpose is to make you wish you had never gotten out of bed in the morning. All these are things that can inflict pain, make one very sick, or just be plain annoying. With some caution and an ever watchful eye one can often avoid a lot of pain and heartache. Even the most cautious person, however, is still subject to unwarranted attacks and troubles, a part of life that can't be avoided. My Mom always told me, "Don't go looking for trouble, plenty of trouble will find you" which I considered pretty good advice. I try not to look for trouble, Pickles on the other hand, finds enough trouble for all of us.

A couple months back, during the peak of lawn mowing season, a little incident happened that was somewhat disturbing and out of the ordinary, even for this area. Mr. Brown had taken on his role of "The Lawn Ranger", happily tending to his mowing duties. I was working on my latest "relocation project", which entailed jerking weeds from the flower beds and slinging them over my back, as well as, digging up a plant from here and moving it over there and moving one from over there to here. As one of my aunts always said, "I've got IBM flowers"- meaning "I've Been Moved". Pickles was busy at the edge of the yard behind me, sniffing for the tantalizing smell of his favorite rabbit. That crusty hardened old hare that runs faster than all the others, eluding him time and time again as he takes Pickles on a wild rabbit chase through briars and brambles. A somewhat special bond exists between the two of them and they both seem to enjoy the chase. So it was that Pickles is behind me, Mr. Brown is mowing in front of me, and I am in the middle....I just love being a middle man. I had just bent over and was tugging with all my might on a nasty little, deep-rooted weed, and Mr. Brown had just shifted into 3rd gear, when I heard Pickles bark behind me. It was a distinct and disturbing bark echoing loud and clear, unlike any I had previously heard from Pickles. From the tone of Pickles' bark I knew immediately that something was wrong.

So it was that I quickly turned to see Pickles running towards me with a coyote right on his tail in hot pursuit. I dropped my garden tools and ran towards them yelling as they continued to run towards me. Pickles and the coyote continued running toward me, and the coyote was so focused on catching his prey that he was oblivious to my theatrics. Finally, the coyote's brain engaged enough for him to realize that there was a screaming human lunatic in rubber boots and shorts running straight towards him waving a garden shovel, and he better alter his route. With a mere 30 feet of distance between us, the coyote made an abrupt turn and was gone in a flash. Pickles was a little shook up, and I have to tell you I was a little unnerved myself. For a coyote to venture that close with me in the yard, the noise of the lawn mower, and the fact that it was mid-day was very out of character. Coyotes tend to be nocturnal, venturing out after dark. I suppose the coyote was so intent on the "meet and eat" with Pickles that he had tuned out any danger and lost common coyote scents (pun intended). While typically fearful of humans, coyotes will kill small pets along with other assorted small animals for food. Dogs have a natural instinct that tells them to avoid coyotes.

Later that evening after things had settled down a bit, Pickles and I discussed the coyote incident. I told him that he had done the right thing by barking out my name and running towards me, "his master". I also told Pickles that God did in fact intervene by allowing me to hear Pickles bark over the roar of the lawn mower...something that would have been difficult in the best of situations but so much more so due to my hearing loss. I then read a couple different verses to Pickles.

Exodus 14:14
The Lord will fight for you, and you shall hold your peace.
I told Pickles it didn't say the Lord may fight for you, it said He "will." He's not going to think about it for a bit, God will jump right in the midst of the fuzz and fur battle.

I thought about my own life in times of attacks and troubles. There are times when I am suddenly in danger and under attack, caught off guard for whatever reason. To try and fight the enemy alone, as well as being so unprepared, would be an unwise and bad choice, but if I will call out God's name and turn or run (so to speak) towards him, then God will be quick to step in and defend me. Too many times I have tried to fight my own battles with no success, all while "my Master" was standing quietly waiting for me to call for help, to acknowledge that I am weak and defenseless on my own, but a force to be reckoned with when God is in control.

Deuteronomy 20:4
For the Lord your God is He who goes with you, to fight for you against your enemies, to save you.

What a great comfort to know God will always (not sometimes) go before me to fight my battles. Regardless of the earthly outcome, as a child of God's, a sinner saved by grace, I will always win.

Proverbs 11:27

He who earnestly seeks good finds favor,
but trouble will come to him who seeks evil.

Howling with the Pack

Several months had passed since a coyote had came into the yard and quite frankly, I had all but forgotten about it. It had been a long day, and Mr. Brown and I were in that deep coma-like sleep at 3:00 A.M. when suddenly Pickles commenced to barking, howling loudly, and running throughout the entire house. Slowing only momentarily when he hit the front door at full throttle and was thrown back into the middle of the room.

Naturally, Mr. Brown and I were both startled awake with adrenaline gushing through our veins with the speed of the waters rushing over Niagara Falls. In approximately 7.8 seconds, I exited a deep slumber, levitated from the bed, flew down the stairs, and was by Pickles' side trying to determine whether we were being invaded by aliens or what other horrible calamity was upon us. Not seeing anything readily set to destroy us, I began to try and wake my mind up enough to evaluate how serious a situation we were in. It was only when Pickles paused to catch his breath that I heard a pack of coyotes running close by the house. It sounded as if there were 4 or 5. They were howling while chasing whatever their nightly supper was going to be. Pickles continued his barking, and howling while demanding to be let outside, for what I have no idea. I very sternly reminded him about the incident several months back in which he was about to become an appetizer had I not intervened. I then told Pickles, in no uncertain terms, to go back to his room and go to bed.

When morning rolled around, it was very clear that Pickles was upset with me over the early morning episode in which I would not let him out. I sent him outside to take care of his morning duties, and when he came back in, still sulking, we sat down to read from the Bible.

Proverbs 14:16
A wise man fears and departs from evil, but a fool rages and is self-confident.

I explained to Pickles that he was being foolish to want to go outside and bark at the coyotes. Not only was he out-numbered, but he was also out-sized and nothing good would come of it from his end. He would be putting not only himself in great danger but also me if I tried to intervene. Why would he want to purposely put himself in harm's way?

How often have I been foolish and walked down a path spiritually, physically, or in relationships that was dangerous thinking that I would have the strength and will power on my own to overcome? But oh, how loving and forgiving God is, that even when I have deliberately put myself in danger He is still quick to defend His child.

Colossians 3:17

And whatever you do in word or deed, do all in the name of the Lord Jesus, giving thanks to God the Father through Him.

Dog Nose

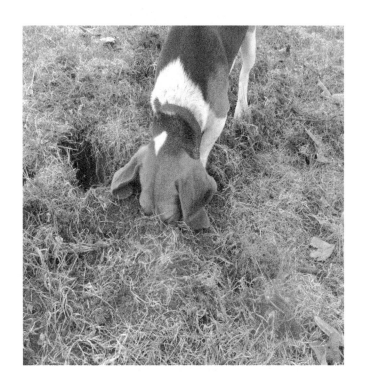

On more than one occasion as a youngster I heard an old timer remark, "That dog sure enough has a nose on him." Young, naive, and not as worldly as I am now, I would look at the dog and determine, "Yes, he does in fact have a nose, don't they all?" It was only when I got older and wiser that I found out the real meaning of, "That dog's got a nose on him." For those of you who like me, were unfamiliar with the meaning of, "that dog sure has a nose on him," I have broken it down into simple layman terms.

Dog nose- Nerb (combination of both noun and verb)

1. The ability to take a cold, wet, black, dog nose (noun) and "cold nose" (verb) a person from behind resulting in screams, leaps, and twirls while running in mid-air. Many a late-night chicken cleaning has resulted from a farmer getting "cold-nosed" from behind after rushing out to check on a ruckus in the chicken coop in the middle of the night.
2. The ability to sniff a cookie crumb lurking under a couch cushion, resulting in shredded cushions in order to get one cookie crumb that is visible only under a microscope.
3. The ability to sniff out a rabbit hiding in the garden from the back room of the house. This phenomenon only occurs after everyone is in bed and asleep for the night. It is typically between the hours of 1:00 A.M. to 3:30 A.M. and is followed by aggressive barking loud enough to be heard at the neighbor's house a mile up the road.
4. The ability to turn off the nose and ignore the smell

of four rabbits happily munching in the garden during the mid-day hours while walking by within six inches of the rabbits.

Pickles has "a nose". His nose can be both good and bad, as well as indifferent on occasion. I have watched him sitting in the yard when suddenly the twitching starts as his nose is detecting the smell of a rabbit that needs to be put back into its perimeter. I have also observed him at the far end of the driveway in a dead run (to who knows where) suddenly throw on his brakes as he smells the piece of candy that I am merely thinking about eating. With the speed of a humming bird, he makes a 180 degree turn and torpedoes a 1/4 mile back to where I am sitting, finishing with a flying leap into my lap all before I have even got the candy out of the wrapper.

One of the most disturbing uses of his nose is his ability to smell a dinosaur bone buried 1500 years ago, 15 feet down, in the middle of the green bean patch. Although the bone has been there all along, it only now becomes an issue when the new green bean plants are in full bloom. The odor is suddenly intensified by the blooming of the beans, making it unbearable for Pickles to ignore. Pickles then proceeds to dig it up with a total disregard for the delicate green bean plants. The dirt that gets impacted up his nose while digging throws his bearings off. This results in his necessity to dig up an area the approximate size of a baseball field.

Interesting how a good talent and gift can go bad if not careful. Pickles and I talked about appropriate uses for his nose and I read to him from the Bible

1 Corinthians 12:4-7
4 There are diversities of gifts, but the same Spirit.
5 There are differences of ministries, but the same
Lord. 6 And there are diversities of activities, but it is the
same God who works all in all. 7 But the manifestation of
the Spirit is given to each one for the profit of all:

Our gifts are not just for ourselves but are meant to
be shared with others, to be used to help someone other
than ourselves and to be a blessing to others as well.
Therefore, Pickles needs to use his nose to keep rabbits
out of the garden. By doing what he is meant to do with
his nose he is being useful to me as God intended.

Some of our gifts and talents are obvious, others are
subtle, but each one is equally important. I know people
that have the ability to see someone in need of help and
know exactly what to do and how to get it done. I've known
others who make phone calls to shut-ins just to say hi and
brighten their day...talk about a great encourager, that
certainly is one. These are all gifts and all ones that I wish
I had, but God gave me other gifts/talents, one of which is
writing. Do I always want to sit down and write? Nope,
but it is an act of obedience when I do. Don't ever under-
estimate yourself. God will take the seemingly ordinary
and make it extraordinary.

1 Corinthians 15:58
Therefore, my beloved brethren, be steadfast,
immovable, always abounding in the work of the Lord,
knowing that your labor is not in vain in the Lord.

End Of The Road

God gave mothers an extra sense, "motherly intuition", or as the country folk say, "I've got a gut feeling something ain't right". When the time comes that all of a mother's children have grown up and left home, that 6th sense goes into a state of hibernation. Although this "motherly intuition" does in fact remain, it will not be as sensitive to subtle changes as it had once been. Upon moving a child or beagle into the home or the arrival of grandchildren, the motherly intuition kicks back in at 100% efficiency. It is this same "gut feeling" that has been a constant in our life since Pickles arrived on the scene. It never seems to go away. This brings me to the latest Pickles escapade.

It is not unusual for Pickles to disappear in the late evening only to return after dark or sometimes even the next morning, at which point he drags in with bloodshot eyes and goes straight to bed with no explanation of where he has been. I no longer bother to ask where he has been or what he has been doing. I figure it's probably best that I don't know, especially if I have not received any angry or threatening phones calls from the neighbors.

A few nights back Pickles pulled the disappearing act again, close to his normal bedtime. Perhaps that is why my gut feeling kicked in, I don't really know, I just know that it did kick in. I also know that if my gut feeling has kicked in where Pickles is concerned it probably is not a good thing...kind of a bad omen, so to speak. Mr. Brown agreed that he also had that gut feeling (could of been the chili he just ate). Two gut feelings at one time only intensified my unease. With all of that in mind, and in the best interest of the neighborhood, I decided to call around and try to locate Pickles.

My calls are based on illogical logic, which is what life with Pickles has become. Knowing where his favorite porch is, it was only natural to call the owners of "Pickles' Porch #1." Their porch was clean and uninhabited, but they would let me know if they spotted him. Just as I was hanging up, I get a phone call from an unknown phone number. When I politely answered, I was greeted with, "Hi, we are calling about Pickles," to which I respond, "What about him?" I really wanted to deny knowing him, but it is my phone number on his dog tag, so it's going to be pretty difficult at this point. I finally confessed that I do know Pickles, and then I am informed that Pickles is at their house which is two miles up the road, which happens to be over a mile out of Pickles' normal roaming range and dangerously close to the highway. I assure them that I am indeed on my way to get the little brat and will be there in about 10 minutes.

I quickly slip on my rubber boots, jump in the truck, and head up the road before Pickles gets much more of a chance to embarrass or humiliate me. I pull in the driveway and a young boy walks towards me with Pickles bouncing along side of him on a leash. Of course, Pickles goes all wild upon seeing me and does the "I'm so glad to see you, I was lost and so scared" act. I know this is a put-on to make himself look good, it's always this same scenario where Pickles is concerned.

I quickly load him in the truck hoping to avoid any further confrontations. Too late, I see the lady of the house come out, and I brace myself. I've been through it before, so I know what's coming. It is never a pleasant experience, and no matter how hard I try I will never get used to it. Those gut feelings I had earlier have now turned into rollings and rumblings of which could put a magnitude 7 earthquake to shame. Then she hits me with it, and I am slammed back against the truck door, pinned tight as she lets loose on me. "Oh my goodness! He is the cutest little dog ever! If I didn't have a dog already we would have just kept him." At this point I casually mention that perhaps her dog would like to have a companion. Pausing long enough to catch her breath she continues her barrage, "I was afraid he wouldn't want to come in the house, but he came on in and made himself at home. He's so precious!"

My mind quickly shifted into overdrive as I began to imagine what kind of garbage he may have consumed as he played the helpless, lost, and starving beagle role that he has perfected. I casually reply, "Thank you, but really, he's a brat." After a few more pleasantries, Pickles and I head back to the house. It's bad enough to hear how cute he is and all, but it's manifested by him laying casually in the truck seat, taking it all in, and getting that smug "How could you possibly be mad at me?" look all over his face.

Of course, when we arrive home, Pickles wants to immediately go to his room (which pretty well describes the whole house in his mind), but I planted him firmly down in my lap and we got the Bible out and read.

1 Corinthians 15:30
And why do we stand in jeopardy every hour?

I tried to tell Pickles that each and every time he leaves our property he is putting himself in danger. You hear it on the news every day, dog-nappers trolling the roads looking for victims, little girls thinking he is adorable and will be cute to dress up, and a multitude of other dog dangers. I know for a fact Pickles can easily be lured into any vehicle with a microscopic crumb of any flavor potato chip.

There are also big dogs looking to eat little dogs, cats with a chip on their shoulder just looking for a dog that they can slash their claws across, and the list goes on and on. Pickles had jeopardized himself, and was very close to even greater danger. Another 1/4 mile and Pickles would have been on the highway, and his beagle brain is not smart enough to understand, in his arrogance, that all those cars flying by at 70 mph will not stop for him...most could not stop if they wanted to. He simply cannot be that far from home. I'm not trying to be mean, I am trying to spare him from being the latest meal on the roadway for the local buzzards. If Pickles wants to remain safe, he has to stay closer to home and follow the rules and boundaries I have set for him. There is no other way for me to protect him.

I was then reminded that likewise I stray off at times and get close to a danger zone. I forget where I am supposed to be, where I am going, and I pretty much do my own thing without thinking of the dangers I may be putting myself in, or the harm I could be causing in my relationship with others or, more importantly, my relationship with Christ. It is so easy to get caught up in the moment and lose sight of the whole picture while I keep chasing whatever is in front of me. Once I veer off the path, satan is quick to step in and make the trail we are running down look fun and pleasing, when in reality it ends with a sudden drop-off into a dark abyss. However, if I stop, look, listen, and turn my heart towards God, He will direct my path back away from the dangers. God didn't lay out rules to cause us to be miserable, quite the opposite. Rules and guidelines are to protect us and enable us to live a much happier, stress-free life. Life is much easier and safer if we follow the rules and guidelines set before us instead of trying to do it our own way.

Beagle Buddies

From seemingly out of nowhere, Pickles hinted around that he would like a "friend"...nothing serious, just someone to share a bowl of Beagle Bits with and maybe chase an occasional rabbit or two. Mr. Brown and I made it very clear that Pickles was not getting a girlfriend...maybe an occasional friend, but nothing more. With that being cleared up, I allowed Pickles to invite three girls over a couple weeks ago for a short visit. He was pretty excited and spent quite some time getting ready...rolling in cow manure and various dead, things as well as eating a wide assortment of unidentifiable things so he would have that stench of dead decaying items that dogs find so irresistible. He then waited in eager anticipation.

The girls finally arrived and it became apparent rather quickly that he was going to strike out. First out of the car was Penelope, the big boisterous type, all about running and having fun, the good-ole-boy type. Penelope was followed by Daffy, the snotty little princess that is not going to be seen with any dog that has not placed at least in the top 5 at the Westminster Dog Show and expects one to jump and attend to her every whim each time she raises her eyebrows. She, in fact, walked right by Pickles with her little snout up in the air and went in the other room, not even acknowledging his existence Then came Trixy, aah, cute little Trixy. Pickles was instantly smitten. Trixy is dainty, cute, and bouncy the ditsy cheerleader type. Clearly, she was the only one in his eyes. He proceeded to swagger up to her, offering her his most prized possession, a piece of shriveled up skin with a little bit of hair attached...the remains of something long since dead and decayed. Trixy eagerly snatched it (whatever it was) from him and immediately she turned into a mean, snarling wolf that smelled blood. Trixy made it very clear that she was not sharing. This unidentifiable prize was all hers and no one else better even think about looking at it, let alone touching it. With a look of shock and hurt, Pickles retreated to the far corner of the property. I felt sorry for him, but it wasn't long before Penelope went running over to engage him in a 10k run throughout the neighborhood, complete with pond wading, cow pie rolling, stick chewing, and gorging on dead things. With all the good, old-fashion fun and dog games with Penelope, Pickles forgot all about cute little Trixy.

Later that evening, after the girls had returned to their home and Pickles had settled in for the evening, I read to him from the Bible.

1 Samuel 16:7
But the Lord said to Samuel, "Do not look at his appearance or at his physical stature, because I have refused him. For the Lord does not see as man sees; for man looks at the outward appearance, but the Lord looks at the heart."

I explained how the one he thought looked so cute and sweet turned out to be a real growling grizzly, but the plain Jane (Penelope) had a kind, fun-loving heart. Plain Jane proved to be a true friend, expecting nothing in return. Daffy wasn't going to be a friend for any reason, and Trixy would be a friend until she got what she wanted and then she would turn on you in a blink and become a ravenous grizzly ready to shred you apart one limb at a time.

I realize I am so guilty of doing the same thing. I judge much too often on outward appearances and circumstances. Many a time I have prayed for God to allow me to see a particular person from His (God's) perspective. This usually is very humbling to me, as well as a real eye opener. Quite often I am then filled with compassion instead of frustration. It is then that I pray to be able to see myself as God sees me. This can be very tough for me to accept, but worthwhile, lest I begin to think too highly of myself. There are other times when satan is attacking me telling me how worthless I am and it is at this point that God can really put it back in perspective and allow me to recognize the good in myself that God sees.

My prayer is that I see others, as well as myself, as God sees us. I have found that God's view of others is much better than my own view. God sees the heart and soul, I am only able to see the outside. This has been such a help to me when I am struggling to understand a difficult person. By seeing myself through God's eyes I can also see how my attitude needs to change.

The Buddies Return

Pickles had some friends over last weekend, three to be exact, accompanied by their people. Of course, Pickles' friends belong to the younger generation, who happen to be a little more lax on the whole discipline issue than we are. Pickles struggles with bad manners enough as it is without having any outside bad influence. Our philosophy is very simple,"We own the house and we rule." Pickles, however, is continually working to turn it around in his favor to "I own the house, and I rule and drool". To be fair, Pickles and his three friends played outside from early morning until after dark running, barking, digging, biting, and rolling in dead things, as well as eating dead things. All those things dogs like to do and which are, for the most part, acceptable. It was when nightfall came that things got sticky and out of control. Pickles is not allowed (nor will he ever be allowed to be) on the bed. No negotiations, no further discussion. Pickles' friends, however, are allowed to be on the bed with their people (not my choice). Up until this point, Pickles had been content to sleep in his own dog bed in the back utility room. Unbeknownst to me, that was all about to change. Sometime after we had turned in for the night, there was a dog party that broke out, and Pickles gained access to the main living area. I am fairly certain in my own mind that Pickles did not hesitate when he was invited in. As we are all aware, if you give a dog an inch they take the bed, couch, chair, anything and everything else, or so they (Pickles) try. Judging from the relocation of pillows and such, I was able to determine that it was free reign all night; if one spot felt too lumpy to sleep, there was always a couch, chair, kitchen table, or you name it.

I spent a week trying to undo bad behavior after this recent visit from Pickles' friends, being careful to explain why he can't do things that others are allowed to do. This has been a tough endeavor, as Pickles had observed it worked out pretty well for his friends.

I tried to explain that the activities and attitudes that his friends were allowed to do were not totally bad, however, Pickles has never been able to exhibit any self-control. I knew therefore he was very likely to keep pushing his limits until he was doing unacceptable things, such as drinking coffee out of my cup, chumming with cats, using my toothbrush, etc. I explained that it was best for him to avoid all the little things that could lead to big things. Pickles and I read several passages from the Bible that I hoped would encourage him. I am pretty sure he understood, but because he is such a strong-willed little dog I'm certain it will be a constant and on going battle for him.

Proverbs 1:15
My son, do not walk in the way with them, keep your foot from their path.

Romans 12:2
And do not be conformed to this world, but be transformed by the renewing of your mind, that you may prove what is that good and acceptable and perfect will of God.

As I was reading this passage, I got to thinking that I have been guilty of the same thing. I do or say things that start out innocent and are okay, all while knowing that it is leading me towards a wrong spiritual path for my life and the plans that God has for me. It is a pathway to actions and situations that I should not be a part of and that will certainly cause me to stumble or worse yet, cause a fellow Christian to falter (or maybe even present a stumbling block to an unbeliever). It is therefore best that I turn away from even the little things that could lead down a path I don't want to go. Each one of us have areas of weakness that we struggle with in our spiritual lives and satan knows what they are. satan will use every tactic to trip us up and encourage us to step past our boundaries into areas that can cause us a lot of grief, as well as stumbling in our spiritual lives. It is so much easier to not take that first step than to have to hike back through life's briars and brambles.

James 1:14-15
14 But each one is tempted when he is drawn away by his own desires and enticed.
15 Then, when desire has conceived, it gives birth to sin; and sin, when it is full-grown, bring forth death.

I cannot continue straddling the fence, leaning from side to side. I have to make a choice to get on one side or the other. It is all too easy to land on the wrong side of the fence. Life is much easier if we stay far away from the fence and pushing against the boundaries.

God is Bigger

A few months back a member of Mr. Brown's family, CJ, arrived at our home for an extended stay. Much to Pickles delight, CJ brought along his dog Simon as a playmate for Pickles. Now Simon is a cute little fluff ball, more fluff than anything else...an important fact that Pickles somehow failed to notice. The moment that Simon jumped out of the truck Pickles was right there to welcome him with a sniff, lick, and a bark. Now, being fluffy, Simon appeared taller and broader than Pickles by several inches, and, as a result, got his bluff in on Pickles. It was only after dominance was established that they played well together, as long as Pickles jumped every time Simon barked. Once that little issue had been resolved, they were off at a dead run. They chased one another, leaping and bounding all over the Brownstead. Pickles and Simon delighted in eating and rolling in dead stuff, digging up the yard, rolling in mud puddles, and numerous other dog activities. They both had a doggone great time and passed out at bedtime snuggled up together.

Fast forward three months later and the weather is beginning to get warm, which means that Simon has just gotten his summer haircut. So it was that once again CJ and Simon arrived for an extended visit at our home. Pickles eagerly ran out to greet Simon as soon as their vehicle stopped in our drive. From where I stood across the yard, I could see Pickles' confusion as he looked at Simon, who was now smaller then Pickles. As this all sank in, Pickles suddenly had the upper hand and was now the dominant dog. It was Simon's turn to jump every time Pickles barked. After they had played and wore down, I explained to Pickles that in his rush to jump in and do his own thing he had not sized up (pun intended) the situation the first time Simon came for a visit. As a result, Pickles had to endure things he shouldn't have during their stay with us...not to mention the constant worried look on his little beagle face. I then got out the Bible and read to Pickles.

Isaiah 41:10

Fear not, for I am with you; Be not dismayed, for I am your God. I will strengthen you, Yes, I will help you, I will uphold you with My righteous right hand.

I explained to Pickles that he had rushed into playing and jumping and did not take time to look over the situation before he allowed Simon to bully him around.

I thought about how many times in my life I took a small problem and blew it up into something big. In my fearful rush, I failed to remember that God is bigger than my problem. Once I let God have control of the situation, I realized how small and insignificant the problem was to begin with...most times more fluff than substance. God is bigger than all our problems.

I love the following acronym for fear that does a good job of putting it all into perspective:

Fear
False
Evidence
Appearing
Real

More often than not, there is a false evidence presented by satan to get us worked up into a frenzied panic. If satan can get us into a fearful and worked-up state, then suddenly our faith and trust has been shaken and he (satan) is getting the upper hand. We are easy to manipulate and control when our "fear factor" is at high alert.

Revelation 1:17
"Do not be afraid; I am the First and the Last"

God has us covered from the beginning of our lives until we take our last breath and every breath in between. When all has fallen around us God will still be on His throne with open loving arms, waiting to pick us up.

Dye Laughing-Colored Hair

I vividly remember the first time I laid eyes on Pickles. He was tiny, cute, cuddly, and innocent looking, or perhaps at that point he was still innocent. We learned soon enough that innocence is not one of his virtues. As Pickles has gotten older he has exhibited signs of ADBD (attention deficit beagle disorder), BBBD (bad behavior beagle disorder) and BDD (beagle defiant disorder). Nothing could have prepared us for life with him. If I tell him no, he is determined he is going to do it anyway. We have had multiple discussions about various behavioral issues with no apparent remorse on his part. What is so frustrating is the fact that he and I will be discussing his bad behavior and I tell him, "If I had it to do over, you wouldn't be here," and he gets that worried beagle look (the wrinkled eyebrows, head tipped up, etc.), which suckers me into thinking he finally understands and then instantly I regret what I have said to him.

From day one, Pickles and I have been in an ongoing battle over the trash can in the bathroom. He loves to get those little Dixie cups (or whatever else he can get his teeth on) out of the trash and shred them into minuscule pieces all over the house. He doesn't contain the shredding to just one room, mind you, but spreads the shred from the front to the back of the house. No room is spared from his shredding frenzy extravaganza. We had been working on this, and I was hopeful we had made great progress in getting over this nasty little annoying habit...but enough of that and onto the real issue.

Based on some loose calculations and observations during my life time, I have come to the conclusion that 1 in every 1.25 women alter their hair color at some point. I am the 1 in every 1.25. Two things about my alterations, 1) I try to keep them subtle and within the normal hair color palette (no greens, purples, blues, etc.), and 2) I make my own color alterations. Now I realize there are some of you who think I do my own hair because I am frugal, but the real truth is that I can't sit still in a beauty shop long enough. At home, I can apply the appropriate hair color and go work in the garden until my timer goes off. Admittedly, on more than one occasion I have startled the UPS man. I'm not sure if it is the oozy-looking goo on my head or the rubber boots-and-shorts-while-carrying-a-shovel combination that gets to him. Apparently therapy was successful, as the UPS man has recovered and once again is delivering to our house although he still has some minor tics. So with that being said, just last week I noticed that my hair tone was getting a little less flattering and figured it was time to spiffy up a bit. I carefully selected a nice soft barnyard blonde and went about my business.

Although I have a bigger brain, I do have a smaller head, so there usually is some of the barnyard blonde coloring left over in the little dispenser...which I drop into the trash can. After careful observation and scrutiny, I felt pretty good about myself the next morning as I left for work. I pull off the barnyard blonde quite well, if I must say so myself.

On this particular morning, I left Pickles in the house with Mr. Brown when I left for work. I figured a little extra beagle/person bonding time would be good for

Pickles and hopefully wouldn't be too traumatic for Mr. Brown.

So it was, that after a long day at work, I headed towards the homestead with a sense of "all is well". The neighbors hadn't called to complain about Pickles and the cops had not been by the office to discuss anything he may have done. I arrived home to the usual blast of a flying, leaping beagle that hits me about neck high, which I am beginning to get accustomed to. After regaining my balance, I notice what appears to be blood on him. Several spots on his body to be exact. I determine it can't be too serious due to his leaping, flying, and gnashing of teeth. However, I do want to examine him to determine what in the world he has gotten into, or what has got a hold of him. The blood seemed to have settled on the ends of the hair shaft which I thought odd. Carefully, I continued to part his hair and look very closely to see if I could find any puncture wounds. At this point, I only became more confused as I am having difficulty determining the source of the blood. Suddenly it all came to me, and I realized he's dyed his hair. The BBBD (bad beagle behavior disorder) had kicked in after I had left for work, and Mr. Brown clearly had not been attentive to what Pickles was doing or getting into. Pickles had been in the trash and gotten hair color on himself. I now have a beagle that has brownish red polka dots in his black hair.

After I recovered from laughing uncontrollably I marched his little polka-dotted self in the house and we read from the Bible.

Luke 12:2-3

2 For there is nothing covered that will not be revealed,
nor hidden that will not be known.

3 Therefore whatever you have spoken in the dark will
be heard in the light, and what you have spoken in the ear
in inner rooms will be proclaimed on the housetops.

I told Pickles I knew what he had done after I had left
for work. He may have thought it was fun and games and
no one would know but his bad behavior was now very
public. He was going to be laughed at by the neighborhood
animals. That ugly, old alley cat was going to have a great
time poking fun and taunting him about his polka dots. I
explained to Pickles that he was going to have to just
suffer through all the teasing and name calling. Not only
had he done something wrong, but he had thought he could
get away with it and no one would notice. It's hard to not
notice a polka-dotted beagle.

I began to reflect on my own life and the times I
thought I was getting by with some little indiscretion. The
truth is God sees all, and often times worse than the
actual indiscretion is my attempt to hide what I have done.
Someone somewhere will see, and at some point it will be
made known. I'm speaking from experience here. I am
going to mess up and make mistakes and do things I
shouldn't. God is not going to disown me, He only wants me
to confess and admit I screwed up, then God is quick to
forgive. It is much easier to step forward and fess up
than wait to be called accountable. We will not be
condemned. We will be forgiven, and it will be forgotten. I

would much rather only need to ask forgiveness for my mistake than for both my mistake and my deceit in trying to hide what I had done.

Psalms 34:22
The Lord redeems the soul of His servants, And none of those who trust in Him shall be condemned.

Jealousy

My transition from working away from home to working at home in some ways has been much easier than I had anticipated and in other ways more difficult. I suppose that this balances things out to a neutral state. Pickles, on the other hand is loving it, and enjoys having me around every day all to himself. He has been quite content to spend more time in the house, keeping tabs on me and what I am doing. Always looking for ways to capitalize on having me there to hand out treats or belly rubs. I, on the other hand, find it rather annoying having him question my every move. It quickly became apparent that Pickles, in his own mind, had divided the house into zones in his attempt to keep track of my every move. As one would suspect, this has become very agitating to me. It works like this, Pickles gets himself situated in close proximity to where I am presently located and commences to fall into a deep, comatose sleep. The minute I move from that zone into another zone, he bursts awake with the speed of sound and relocates to his coordinating zone. On those occasions when I venture out of all of his zones, he is quick to appear at my side. Pickles carries this sudden appearing maneuver out so swiftly and quietly it is unnerving to me. It is like "poof" there he is appearing from thin air with that, "Where are you going? What are you doing?" accusatory look that I have become so accustomed to.

I had finally come somewhat to terms with this new behavior and was learning how to best deal with it when Pickles' poodle pal, Simon, came for a visit. Simon had not been to visit since I had made the switch from working away from home to working at home. There was no reason for me to suspect anything would be different between Simon and Pickles. From my perspective, nothing had changed…clearly an unrealistic thought process on my part, which left me ill-prepared and caught off guard for the mayhem that soon ensued.

Jealousy broke forth in the highest form, much like "Old Faithful" erupting in Yellowstone Park. Pickles and Simon instantly became like two teenage football players fighting over their most cherished, beloved cheerleader. One or the other merely had to glance my direction, and a beagle brawl would immediately break out. Growling, leaping, biting, shoving, kicking, and hair pulling, Pickles and Simon were utilizing every known (and some unknown) tactic in an attempt to establish ownership of me and win my favor. I dared not speak or make eye contact with either one of them. Had it been a one-time brawl, I may have been able to get a grip on it, but it continued on all day, every day, for the entire week that Simon visited, stopping only at bed time.

During the course of the week I made a trip to town to conduct business as well as get away from all the dog fighting at home. I left the two brawling bullies with Mr. Brown, hoping it would not get out of control while I was gone. Upon my return I was informed by Mr. Brown that, "While you were away the boys did play," as in no fighting, just happy dog frolicking. However, the moment I arrived back on the scene all pandemonium broke out once again. The extraordinary intensity of the situation was mind boggling to me and left me exhausted and unnerved to say the least. I was becoming very anxious for Simon to go home so I could regain some control of my life again.

At some point Simon and Pickles did agree that they would share my lap each morning while I drank my coffee. Of course, the last thing I wanted was two dogs in my lap while I am drinking my hot-enough-to-scald-the-hair-off-your-tongue morning coffee. However, having a few moments where they had called a truce and "cease bark" was in some ways worth sharing my lap. Once coffee time was over, they were back at it with a new vengeance. I wish I could say that it ended well, but it did not end until Simon went home.

It was some time before I could regain my composure enough to chat with Pickles about his behavior. As we chatted, I told Pickles that jealousy, if not brought under control, leads down an ugly path in which innocent people can be hurt spiritually, mentally, and physically. There is no end to the damage that can be done by a jealous person. Pickles was going to risk losing his best friend for no reason. I gently reminded Pickles that he's still my number one beagle, that fact had not changed. I had made it a point to not play favorites and to treat both Pickles and Simon equally while Simon was visiting. I wanted Simon's visit here to be fun and happy. I explained to Pickles also about being selfish and the need to share and then I read from the Bible.

James 3:16
For where envy and self-seeking exist, confusion and every evil thing are there.

Proverbs 27:4

Wrath is cruel and anger a torrent, But who is able to stand before jealousy?

I explained to Pickles that he had allowed his jealousy to turn ugly with all the fighting and biting. Someone was going to get hurt, physically and emotionally because a good friendship was going to be destroyed.

As luck would have it, I had recently ran across a great quote that I read to Pickles. It was a quote that sums up the ugliness of jealousy. I wish I knew who to credit as they certainly hit the nail on the head so to speak.

"Jealousy is a form of hatred built upon insecurity."

Jealousy is a very powerful emotion that fuels a large portion of how we act and react. I admit I have struggled with jealousy and still do, especially when I see others that seem to have no problems navigating life and achieving success. I immediately want to find their flaws and bring them to the attention of everyone around, which brings me back to the Bible.

Matthew 7:3

And why do you look at the speck in your brother's eye, but do not consider the plank in your own eye?

I hate to admit to it but I have had a lot of practice with spotting the "specks" in other's eyes. To be quite honest, I am not sure how I spotted the specks around the planks in my own eyes.

If we look in the Old Testament, there are countless stories of how jealousy fueled anger to the point of murder. It started back in the very beginning. In Genesis Chapter 4, Cain was jealous of Abel's gift to God and killed his brother, and in Genesis Chapter 37, Joseph was sold into slavery by his own brothers because they too were jealous.

The strongest case for jealousy is recorded in the New Testament

Matthew 27:18
For He (Jesus) knew that they had handed Him over because of envy.

The high priests were jealous because Jesus had a following. The high priests would stop at nothing to get rid of Jesus, an innocent man. They feared their jobs may be in jeopardy, or perhaps it would be found out that they themselves did not have their hearts aligned with God. They would stop at nothing, false accusation or whatever it took. They needed to be rid of this guy named Jesus because He had a bigger following.

I have seen jealousy destroy what were once happy and close families. Jealousy very quickly mutates into total, dark, ugly evilness if not reined in and kept under control. One cannot ignore jealousy, it must be dealt with swiftly.

Christ loves each one of us equally, regardless. We have nothing to offer Christ except ourselves. Christ only asks that we ABC it:

Accept Him as our savior

Believe that He gave His life and died on the cross and arose

Commit our hearts and lives to Him.

Ephesians 4:32
And be kind to one another,
tenderhearted, forgiving one another, even
as God in Christ forgave you.

Locked out in the Cold

Mr. Brown and I live in a vintage farmhouse complete with charm, character, and an occasional critter that somehow sneaks in through a crack or crevice... unconventional uniqueness with just the right touch of Bohemian country to balance out the sophisticated appearance. Prior to this year I had not concerned myself with the whole door locking mechanism. However, in May, as Mr. Brown was preparing for his annual Canadian fishing trip (without me), I felt I needed a little more security. I think it was the nastiness of the presidential campaigns combined with all the news media reporting of Russians hacking their way in that concerned me. Taking all this into consideration, I requested a dead-bolt to be installed on the front entrance door. Due to the eclectic blend of old, new, and ancient in our home, I determined it would need to be placed low on the door, and I wanted a dead bolt that slides, not a chain type. With the same loving grumbling I am accustomed to, Mr. Brown complied, and I could now bolt up.

Those who are close to me know that I am a routine person, and my mornings are extremely regimented. One would think I had spent time in the military, perhaps even as a lifer. I assure you I have no military background. I can be flexible when needed, as evidenced by the recent adjustments in my morning routine in order to accommodate the ever-changing demands of Pickles. I have a winter schedule and super-cold winter schedule, as well as spring, summer, and fall schedule. The super-cold winter schedule involves starting my truck to allow it to warm up before I leave for work, whereas a regular winter schedule does not require this additional step. With that being said, it was on one of these super-cold winter days, when Pickles was in the house for his morning visit, that the following event unfolded. You need to understand that Pickles has a tendency to flip out if I step outside without him. I don't know if he thinks I am running away or sneaking out to eat a snack without him, but for whatever reason he gets all excited, bouncing and ricocheting off the furniture, windows, doors, etc. So it was on this coldest of cold mornings that I made a hasty dash out in the subzero temperature to start my truck. Since the whole process takes about 12.3 seconds to complete, I do not deem it necessary to put on coat, hat, or gloves. It is a quick, in and out procedure. On this particular morning as I stepped out the door, I instantly heard Pickles begin the ricochet routine, ending at the front door. I quickly started my truck and raced back to the house, nearly ripping my arm off as I jerked on the door. I yanked on an unyielding door that was locked. It seems that when Pickles hit the door in his ricocheting routine it started a chain reaction in which the dead bolt slid over, locking me out.

I was now standing outside in short sleeves with no coat, hat or gloves, looking in the window at Pickles, who was sitting in the warm dining room with either a worried beagle look or smug beagle look (they are hard to tell apart). Mr. Brown, meanwhile, was in the bathroom getting ready for work, oblivious to the fact that his dear wife was locked outside shivering, pounding on the door, and yelling. I have since determined that the colder you get the louder you can yell and pound. Finally, Mr. Brown came strolling out of the facilities, looked out the window, and wanted to play 20 questions. "Why are you outside without a coat? Is your truck running? Why did you leave Pickles inside? Is my lunch packed? Are you cold?" I'm yelling the same response to each question, "Just open the door and let me in, then we will talk!" After a few moments (which seemed liked hours out in the Antarctic) of the game 20 questions, along with answering questions to prove my identity, Mr. Brown slowly walked to the front door and let me in. Pickles was ecstatic and immediately went into the leaping, bouncing, and ricocheting routine all over again and all over me. I struggled with being upset with Pickles because I felt that perhaps it was not intentional. I decided I didn't want him to suffer anxiety, so I chalked it up to a mere accident on his part. That's what I keep telling myself anyway, who knows.

So, I gave him a little pat on the head and scratched his ears and then read to him.

Proverbs 12:25
Anxiety in the heart of man causes depression, But a good word makes it glad.

Aren't we all guilty of being anxious at times? I know I am, and all it takes is a reassuring word or a pat on the back to quiet my heart. I wonder how often I also overlook those who need a comforting word or touch.

Psalms 46: 1-11

1 God is our refuge and strength, A very present help in trouble.

2 Therefore we will not fear, Even though the earth be removed, And though the mountains be carried into the midst of the sea;

3 Though its waters roar and be troubled, Though the mountains shake with its swelling.

4 There is a river whose streams shall make glad the city of God, The holy place of the tabernacle of the Most High.

5 God is in the midst of her, she shall not be moved; God shall help her, just at the break of dawn.

6 The nations raged, the kingdoms were moved; He uttered His voice, the earth melted.

7 The Lord of hosts is with us; The God of Jacob is our refuge.

8 Come, behold the works of the Lord, Who has made desolation's in the earth.

9 He makes wars cease to the end of the earth; He breaks the bow and cuts the spear in two; He burns the chariot in the fire.

10 Be still, and know that I am God; I will be exalted among the nations, I will be exalted in the earth!

11 The Lord of hosts is with us; The God of Jacob is our refuge. Selah

How often have I gotten upset with someone over some silly little incident, when in all honesty they were doing their best? Accidents happen, we do not live in a perfect world. I want to do a good job and please others, things just go haywire at times. I must remember that God is always present, always near to us. I pray that I become much more attentive to those around me who might just need a pat on the back, a hug, or perhaps just a warm, genuine smile.

Look Up

It was a warm and lazy Sunday afternoon with temperatures just perfect for relaxing on the balcony. Mr. Brown and I were happily sipping our cup of coffee while sharing a chocolate almond candy bar. As we sat there sipping, snacking, making small talk, and enjoying the beauty of the moment, we happened to notice Pickles strolling around in the yard below us. It was interesting to watch Pickles zig-zagging everywhere, totally oblivious to our whereabouts.

After a few moments of silent observation, Mr. Brown and I decided to add another element of fun. We quietly called out Pickles' name. This proved to be quite entertaining as we watched him throw on the brakes, stiffen up, and cock his head to the side with his tail straight up. The moment he let his guard down, we spoke his name again. Pickles looked forward, backwards, to the right, to the left, and down, but not once did he look up to the source of his spoken name. Finally, I stood to clearly make myself visible to Pickles. Instantly, Pickles was at ease and let his tail wag in delighted relief at finally finding the location of his master.

Pickles and I talked later about hearing your master call your name and how we should respond. I scratched Pickles behind the ears and told him he did a good job hearing his master speak his voice and stopping to listen and look. Pickles and I then read from the Bible that night.

John 10:27-29
27 My sheep hear My voice, and I know them, and they follow Me.

28 And I give them eternal life, and they shall never perish; neither shall anyone snatch them out of My hand.
29 My Father, who has given them to Me, is greater than all; and no one is able to snatch them out of My Father's hand.

Psalms 121:1-8
1 I will lift up my eyes to the hills-- From whence comes my help?
2 My help comes from the Lord, Who made heaven and earth.
3 He will not allow your foot to be moved; He who keeps you will not slumber.
4 Behold, He who keeps Israel shall neither slumber nor sleep.
5 The Lord is your keeper; The Lord is your shade at your right hand.
6 The sun shall not strike you by day, Nor the moon by night.
7 The Lord shall preserve you from all evil; He shall preserve your soul.
8 The Lord shall preserve your going out and your coming in from this time forth, and even forevermore.

This got me to thinking about how as a child of God I often fail to look up and listen to God when I have a problem. Instead, I tend to look for an answer to my problem from other earthly sources first, and finally, as a last resort, I look up to God. God always has the perfect answer and solution to whatever I am going through.

1 Kings 19:12
and after the earthquake a fire, but the Lord was not in the fire; and after the fire a still small voice.

God speaks our names quietly. Don't look around, look up, be still, and listen.

Mouse Hunting

I have been receiving photos of Pickles lately from various locations around the neighborhood, and it is apparent that he leads a whole different life beyond the perimeter of the Brownstead.

I have, in fact, come to the conclusion that Pickles is indeed trainable, although he continues to remain stubborn as he wanderlusts all over the neighborhood. Prey-driven is the other trait that Pickles has seemingly excelled in. It was not long after Pickles had acquired us that he had a run-in with a neighborhood barn cat that had turned ugly. Pickles and I had a very lengthy discussion about cats and the potential for a lot of unpleasantness. Cats are known to carry grudges for years, always looking for the perfect opportunity to extract revenge on the unsuspecting. I cautioned Pickles to make every attempt within reason to get along with that nasty old hairball. Apparently he listened for once and has gone above and beyond in doing his part.

Photographic evidence has shown that Pickles has in fact chummed up with the cat across the road. Pickles has taken it to a whole new level having added mouse hunting to his repertoire of skills...going so far as to enlist the help of the old barn cat and train under his watchful eye. You could have knocked me over with a feather when I looked at the photos of Pickles and the barn cat happily hunting together. I have to admit that I was a little bit proud of him, as he did seek out a knowledgeable mouse hunter to take mouse hunting lessons from. Of course, he has not bothered to use those skills around here. He has been too busy "wander-lusting" all over the neighborhood.

I scratched Pickles ears and told him I was proud of him for seeking guidance and then we read from the Bible

James 1:5-6
5 If any of you lacks wisdom, let him ask of God, who gives to all liberally and without reproach, and it will be given to him. 6 But let him ask in faith, with no doubting, for he who doubts is like a wave of the sea driven and tossed by the wind.

How much easier our lives would be if we asked God for wisdom instead of waiting until after we have made a mess. I have a tendency to try and handle a difficult situation on my own, asking for help or guidance only after the fact. God clearly tells us to ask and it will be given. I know I need to set pride aside and humble myself to ask for help from the one true God, the ultimate authority on all things. God always has the perfect and correct answer in things both big and small.

Psalms 4:8

I will both lie down in peace, and sleep; For You alone, O Lord, make me dwell in safety.

Now I Lay Me Down to Sleep

Pickles was a spur of the moment, unplanned addition to our family, much like an unexpected and surprise pregnancy after your kids have grown, left home, and blessed you with grand kids. It just happened. As one must do, we have tried to make the best of "that" moment. A moment of unprotected passion in which we paused and lingered a little too long, quickly being seduced by innocent little beagle faces, losing all common sense in the heat of the moment and forgetting all the consequences this sudden decision would have on our lives for years to come.

We are now well into year two of surrendering our lives to one small beagle. Despite all the disturbances he has caused here and throughout the neighborhood, there has always been one area that he has excelled - bedtime. From that very first night, bedtime has been smooth and easy.

Since Pickles was an unplanned life event, I was unprepared for his first night, and did not have a proper beagle bed for him. Making do the best I could I was able to piece together a cute little bed from some extra pillows and blankets that I had on hand. I tucked Pickles in and gave him a little bedtime snack, assuring him we would take good care of him. We heard nothing from him all night. Of course, when I sleep, I hear nothing, so for all I knew his half of the house could have blown away. The next morning I was up early, eager to check on the little tyke. My first glance towards his little bed turned up empty, he was not in it. My eyes quickly swept the room a second time, and then I spotted him curled up in a plastic ice cream bucket. It was one of those heart-tugging moments that took my breath away, pure precious innocence. From the ice cream bucket, Pickles graduated rather quickly to a milk pail for inside napping and a flower pot for those outside naps (with a complete disregard for the flower that was growing in the pot. Pickles seemed content with his bed choices, but I knew he would soon out grow the milk pail. I needed to come up with a permanent sleeping arrangement, and at the rate he was growing, it would need to be pretty quick. It was back at the same flea market where we were acquired by Pickles that I found the perfect, soft, fluffy bed. Pickles loved his new bed, and I was happy to get my bucket back.

The entire first year bedtimes were pleasant with no back barking or stalling around. I would tell Pickles to get in his bed and he would obediently go to his room and get in bed. I always gave him a bedtime snack after he was in bed, and a pat on the head. He was happy, I was happy, everyone was happy. The second year saw an even better bedtime routine, one in which Pickles would go to bed when he got tired, without being told. On occasion he would stay up with us, but more often than not, he was in bed by 8:30 or 9:00. I was delighted with his earlier bedtime, as it gave me some freedom from him being underfoot as I attended to things in the house. Pickles also began to sleep later in the mornings, which is good also, especially since I no longer work away from home. I am an early riser, and it's nice that I don't have him underfoot wanting to know what I am doing, am I going anywhere today, what's for breakfast, and so on and so forth.

Without warning, and rather suddenly, things began to change recently. Pickles was subtle at first, becoming more blatant and bold as time went on. It started in the spare bedroom when I began to notice the covers on the bed were a little bit messy from time to time. A couple of mornings it appeared that the pillows had been rearranged. Then came the morning when I passed by and peered in to see Pickles casually lounging on the bed with the covers turned back and the pillows propped all around him. He didn't seem the least bit concerned when I confronted him about it, actually seeming surprised that I would even question him. His attitude was one of, "Why are you surprised? I sleep here whenever I want." Somehow we managed to get this conflict resolved (or so I thought), and Pickles was back to his normal bedtime schedule sleeping in his own beagle bed. It was when I was away for a couple nights that things once again changed and began to further escalate.

Pickles has never been quiet running up and down the stairway, so it has never been a surprise to us when he is either going up or down. Generally, he sounds like Mr. Moose crashing through the forest chasing after Miss Moose. If the noise were not enough to alert us, the shaking of the light fixtures is a dead give away to his whereabouts. It was while I was gone overnight that Mr. Brown awoke from a sound sleep to hear Pickles thundering up the steps. Mr. Brown told Pickles to get back to his room, and surprisingly, Pickles was obedient doing as he was told, for the moment anyway. Pickles also has the added ability to tip-toe and sneak around quietly when it is in his best interest. Therefore, Mr. Brown woke up the next morning, and there, in the floor, at the foot of the bed was Pickles. I was not there, but I do know there were some words exchanged between them. After I returned from my overnight stay, Pickles seemed to settle back down. There was a week of normalcy (as normal as it can be with Pickles in the household) before Pickles went rogue once again. It was getting close to Pickles' normal bedtime, and he was being his annoying, hyper, pre-bedtime self when suddenly,with no warning, he shot up the stairs. Pickles did not try to keep it quiet as he blasted up the stairs and onto our bed. Within the thirteen seconds it took for me to get upstairs to retrieve him, he had already rearranged the covers and pillows to suit himself and was tucked in. After a short verbal altercation, I marched him back down the stairs. He settled in with one of his chew toys, and Mr. Brown and I continued our conversation. Thirty minutes later Mr. Brown and I realized that Pickles was missing – he had pulled the slinking tip-toeing up the stairs and was sound asleep...on our bed. Every night was now turning into a bedtime battle. Pickles was determined that our bed belonged to him, and he made no bones about it. I also was concerned that Pickles was so determined to do something that he had been told not to do. He started out being sneaky but then became bold and blatant. We had a long talk, and I read to him from the Bible.

Hebrews 4:13
and there is no creature hidden from His sight, but all things are naked and open to the eyes of Him to whom we must give account.

I explained to Pickles that he may have been getting by doing things he shouldn't with me, but God saw every bunny he chased, knew where every bone was that he buried, and knew every bed he had slept on.

James 4:17
Therefore, to him who knows to do good and does not do it, to him it is sin.

I told Pickles that I knew that he knew it was wrong to get on our bed. Even if he had not known, I had supplied him with the knowledge of his wrong doing but he choose to ignore my instructions, making his whole indiscretion a lot worse. However, I did reassure him that he could change his ways, and I certainly would forgive him.

1 John 1:9
If we confess our sins, He is faithful and just to forgive our sins and to cleanse us from all unrighteousness.

I thought about my own life, and how I have at times snuck around and did something that I knew was not right. I felt a twinge of guilt, but since I didn't get caught, I continued. It may not have been a huge infraction (so to speak), but some little something that really I shouldn't be doing. After all, if I am sneaking around to do something, it's a pretty good indicator I am doing something I shouldn't. Over a period of time, it becomes comfortable and suddenly I don't try to hide what I am doing. This is when I have gone too far and intentionally sinned.

Sometimes the thing I am doing is not as bad as trying to hide and cover it up. Not only is this bad for my relationship with Christ, it also may cause someone else to stumble. It is so easy to get caught up in doing what we want to do without considering how it may affect someone else, especially in their Christian walk. When I start sneaking around, I have shifted my focus from Christ to myself, being selfish, desiring only what I want, and thinking only of myself. Nothing is done in secret, even if no one else sees us and what we are doing, God sees all and also sees the intent of our hearts.

Ecclesiastes 4:9-10

9 Two are better than one, Because they have a good reward for their labor. 10 For if they fall, one will lift up his companion. But woe to him, who is alone when he falls. For he has no one to help him up again.

Potato Chips and a Golf Cart

As mentioned before, I tend to be a very regimented person with a strict and mostly unwavering morning routine. Pickles is a fly-by-the-seat-of-your-pants, bratty beagle. Every day is a different day for him, with just enough routine thrown in to totally confuse me. From my many months of observations, I have determined that this is not a good combination.

I start out the same every morning. I get up, plug the coffee pot in, let Pickles outside, then I pour my cup of coffee, and (weather permitting) sit on the balcony and embrace the beauty of the morning, while sipping my cup of coffee. Some days Pickles comes back in, some days I hear him chasing a rabbit as I leave for work, and then there are those days I have no idea where he disappears to. He can stay gone all day with no reported sightings of him. I used to wonder where, what, and why, but I no longer let worried thoughts about him occupy my mind. It's pointless. I remind myself that Pickles belongs to God, and therefore I should let God keep an eye on him. I do wonder though, does *God get tired of keeping tabs on Pickles?*

This particular morning started out routine...coffee on, Pickles out, Pickles in. Then things changed, and Pickles was once again out and gone. As I left for work there were no sightings of him anywhere, which is not unusual. He will either show back up or some other poor soul will have him take up residence at their house, in which case I am off the hook until they get tired of him and realize he has a dog tag on with a phone number. I can't tell you how often I have thought of either changing my phone number or removing his ID tag.

We are fortunate to live near the end of a dead-end county road. Traffic is not an issue. Those who do live here are aware that there is a beagle on the loose. This morning was no different as I headed off to work...that is, until I get a mile up the road. I round a sharp curve, and there, coming towards me, is Pickles. He's smack dab in the middle of the road trotting nonchalantly back in the general direction of the house, not a care in the world. I stop the car, open the door, and mention his name. Okay, really I yell his name and say, "Pickles! What are you doing here? Get in the car now!" He responded exactly as I had expected he would, he turned and wandered off into the edge of the woods, ignoring me the whole way. Needing to get to work, I don't have time to chase him, not that I would have had any luck anyway. I let him go. I figured since he was headed back towards the house that he will continue on that way and probably stop and hang out with his friend Noah for a while before continuing on home.

As I am driving home from work that afternoon, I slow down to wave at Emily, the neighbor girl (age 12), who is driving around in her golf cart. Startled by what I thought I saw, I slammed on my brakes to take a second look, and sure enough, it's Pickles. He's riding around in the golf cart with her, and they are sharing a bag of potato chips. Not the snack size bag either, it's the big family size bag of chips and it's nearly empty at this point. That brat. I pull over, stop and yell for him to come. Naturally, Pickles is not the least bit interested in leaving the remaining potato chip crumbs to come home (or anywhere) with me under any circumstances for that matter. After a couple moments of ugliness, I load him in the truck and drive us home. Of course, Pickles is bloated up like an over-ripe watermelon from all the salt in the chips, and all he wants is to lay around groaning for the remainder of the evening. I assure you there was no sympathy from me. I told Pickles that had he eaten just a few chips it would have been okay, but he did not have the will power to stop. His lack of will power is why I have rules for him (all of which he ignores). They are rules to protect him. I got the Bible out and we began to read.

1 Kings 2:3
And keep the charge of the Lord your God: to walk in His ways, to keep His statues, His commandments, His judgments, and His testimonies, as it is written in the Law of Moses, that you may prosper in all that you do and wherever you turn

Once again, I began to think about my own life and how I don't always like to follow rules. I know from personal experience that life is always easier when I do follow the rules. God didn't make rules just to make us miserable and unhappy, quite the opposite. Rules are to protect us and provide a clear conscience, so we can live free from the burden that disobedience places on us. Whether that burden is a bloated beagle belly from too many potato chips or fear of getting caught doing something else we should have avoided. I'm sure it hurts God to see us suffer as a result of our disobedience, but if we are to learn anything from our mistakes, it is sometimes necessary to suffer the consequences. If I submit to God, He will protect me, and I will prosper according to God's perfect plan for my life.

2 Timothy 4:7

I have fought the good fight, I have finished the race, I have kept the faith.

Runaway

The unexpected warm beginning of November had given me ample time to be at Pickles every beck and call whenever he wanted to play fetch, tug of war, bite, slobber or leap. Not having anything pressing to accomplish, I decided to devote some extra play time and attention to Pickles. We were sitting at the edge of the driveway playing whatever he wanted and having what I thought was a good time when suddenly Pickles stopped, looked at me, turned around and ran off. Now I don't mean he just went a little ways, he packed up and headed south at a get out of Dodge run, headed to Florida by the way it looked. No amount of yelling and calling would slow him down. It beats the life out of me what was going through his beagle brain at that moment, or any other moment for that matter. One minute we are playing and having a good time and the next thing I know he is heading out of here, his legs churning as fast as they will go. I don't know where he went, who he saw, or what he did, but he eventually returned home (about supper time to be exact)... casually strolling in as if nothing had happened. I will be the first to admit that his rejection hurt my feelings. Rejection happens in life, but to be rejected by your own dog is quite humiliating.

Then I thought about my relationship with God. Everything seems to be going good and suddenly I turn and walk away from God. God didn't move or turn away from me, I turned away and moved from Him. God allows me to have a free will, and, as such, will not drag me back nor force Himself into my life. For whatever illogical reason, I sometimes think there is something better, or that I can do it on my own. It is only after I have messed things up that I turn back to God and find that He is right where He always was. Waiting with open arms and no condemnation, God is full of grace and abounding in love. His heart is delighted when I return. God does not shame or ridicule me for leaving in the first place, He is rejoicing over me. The angels in turn do the happy dance that I am back.

Zephaniah 3:17
"The LORD your God in your midst,
The Mighty One, will save;
He will rejoice over you with gladness,
He will quiet you with His love,
He will rejoice over you with singing."

Once I got over my hurt feelings, I informed Pickles I was going to take his name tag off and he could just go ahead and run off. Then we sat down and read about Jonah trying to run away from God, and it didn't work out too well for Jonah. Jonah was finally swallowed up by a whale. Three days in the belly of a whale allowed Jonah plenty of time to think about his life. Jonah had no peace in his heart because he had run away from God. As a result, there were those around Jonah that had no peace either and suffered the consequences. Pickles seemed to enjoy the story about Jonah, although he doesn't want to drink out of the pond anymore.

I did let Pickles know that I was glad he came back before I read to him. Just because he had rejected me was not a reason for me to make Pickles feel rejected.

Joel 2:13
So rend your heart, and not your garments; Return to the Lord your God, for He is gracious and merciful, slow to anger, and of great kindness; And He relents from doing harm.

I love that part that says, "He is gracious and merciful". What a promising comfort for me when I have strayed. I don't have to hang my head in shame or reproach. God will not shame me; His arms are open as wide as "east to west", and I bet a smile brighter than the sun is on His face as He welcomes me back.

When we step away from the "Sonshine" (Christ), we have moved from the true source of light and are stepping into dark territory. It may only be "Sondown" to begin with but as we move further away we very easily can slip into total darkness. The "Sonshine" remains steadfast, exactly where He has always been....never dimming.

Simon

Frequently, Mr. Brown and I have the pleasure of a family member staying with us for an extended time. CJ lives out of state and also owns property adjacent to ours. It is only logical that he stays with us while visiting the area and checking on his farm. On his most recent visit, CJ brought along his dog, Simon. Simon is a cute, rag-mop type of dog that is very mannerly...something that Pickles is not. Once Simon and Pickles had sized one another up and declared dominance the two of them hit it off. Running, jumping, rolling in dead stuff, biting, nipping, barking and finally napping together. Pickles and Simon were having a glorious time. Best friends in the dog world.

Everything seemed to be going well between the two of them until the next morning when Simon happened upon a bone that Pickles had set aside. To be quite honest, Pickles had forgotten all about that bone. Simon promptly ceased playing with Pickles, snatched up that bone and disappeared. Pickles was beside himself, he didn't necessarily want the bone but he sure didn't want Simon to have it. Simon can be his friend but not have his bone, and would I please get his bone back for him. I could see that Pickles had a lot to learn about being a good friend, so I sat him down and told him the story of my best friend.

Lisa and I were best friends from grade school on through high school and even to this day are the very best of friends. Lisa knows things about me that no one else knows and vice versa. She and I shared a locker in high school because we were best friends, and that is what "besties" do. Lisa did have a major flaw that I had to overlook in order for our friendship to work. Lisa loved (more than me) tuna fish sandwiches and bananas, (the rotten black ones). In fact, she ate a tuna sandwich and banana for lunch everyday during our 7th, 8th, and 9th grade years.

We didn't have lunch boxes with ice packs that kids have today. Our lunch was packed in a brown paper bag, and our mom's never worried about food poisoning lurking in our lockers. As a result, our locker stunk. Put a blindfold on and you could sniff your way back to our locker.

Five years after our graduation, I happened to go back and you could still smell the lingering odor of tuna fish and banana in that particular section of the hallway. It seems that several attempts at fumigating that area had failed, and, short of demolishing that segment of the building, the school board had decided to let nature take its course in hopes that one day the odor would fade away.

And so it was, that I had to overlook this flaw in order to maintain our friendship. Lisa was, and still is to this very day, my best friend and worth the odor. I suppose I could have insisted on her not eating tuna and bananas, but that would have been selfish on my part and not being a very good friend...especially since she never said anything about my melty chocolate candy bar oozing over on her homework. Melty????... well, this was also before kids got wimpy and had to have air conditioners in the school.

I explained to Pickles that we may not like, everything about our friends, and they may do things we don't like but we are to love them anyway. Friendship requires us to be givers, and I reminded Pickles that good and loyal friends are hard to come by and should be cherished, by giving up our way of doing things, giving up our time, and giving up our bones when needed. How many things do we do that God doesn't like, but He loves us anyway?

Then I read to Pickles from the Bible.

1 Corinthians 13:4-7
4 Love suffers long and is kind; love does not envy; love does not parade itself, is not puffed up;
5 does not behave rudely, does not seek its own, is not provoked, thinks no evil;
6 does not rejoice in iniquity, but rejoices in the truth;
7 bears all things, believes all things, hopes all things, endures all things.

Then I began to think about how patient God is with me, even when I am a selfish, demanding person (which is quite frequently), and so undeserving.

Sometimes God lets me have my own way and then I find out I'm not quite as smart as I thought I was, and my way is not the best. God is the greatest giver of all, He gave His Son to die for our sins. God is our best friend, always ready to listen to all our problems, ready to remind me that I am worthy. Looking past my faults to see only the good.

I reminded Pickles that he needed to remember to treasure Simon as a friend.

Proverbs 18:24
A man who has friends must himself be friendly, But there is a friend who sticks closer than a brother.

I also told Pickles that he needed to pick his friends very carefully, making certain that they have the same set of values that we do. A wrong friendship can result in a lot of heartache down the road and lead him astray.

Proverbs 22:24-25
24 Make no friendship with an angry man, And with a furious man do not go, 25 Lest you learn his ways and set a snare for your soul

1 Chronicles 16:34
Oh, give thanks to the Lord, for He is good!
For His mercy endures forever.

Snack Snob

One of the things, as in the only thing, that I have managed to inadvertently teach Pickles is that if he comes into the kitchen and sits in front of the spice cabinet he will be rewarded with a snack. It started out innocently enough with Pickles receiving a snack when he came in from outside. It was not long before he figured out this was a pretty good deal and began running in one door and out the other. It didn't take me too long to determine where his extra poundage was coming from either.

On occasion, I would "treat treat" him, meaning I would give him an extra special treat...perhaps a small bite of peanut butter, a tiny bite of bacon, or something else special. From this small act of being extra nice, Pickles went on to being very discriminating about his snacks. I am still trying to determine his reasoning on this and so far, cannot determine what his criteria is. Most of the time he will eat the little dog bone that I offer him, but then comes those times when he feels "entitled". Pickles is not going to eat the snack I am offering and lets me know rather quickly that my offering is substandard. His head is turned to the side, nose up in the air with an attitude. It's a total example of rejection when he averts his eyes and sticks that snout up in the air off to the side. It is up to me at this point to discern what it is that he wants.

Perhaps his dog bone needs a small dollop of peanut butter on it or some other delicacy. To be rejected by one's own beagle is quite demeaning and humbling to say the least.

It was when Pickles had his first birthday that I decided to be generous and indulged him with a spoonful of ice cream. I will not do that again. I have never witnessed a more over-the-top, excited, out-of-control dog in my life. Pickles was ready to shred the refrigerator, throw me to the wolves, or whatever it took to get another bite of ice cream. He was like a junkie in need of another high.

Soon after the ice cream incident, I made the mistake of walking into a different room where the pantry is located and got out a jar of coconut oil to use in a recipe I was working on. Recently I had read that coconut oil is good for dogs, and in fact, if given to a dog regularly can help repel fleas and ticks (I don't know for sure if it works). I gave Pickles a bite of coconut oil thinking nothing of it. This one small isolated incident has now become another of his snack options. When Pickles wants a bite of coconut oil, he will walk into the kitchen and sit down in the normal snack spot. When I arrive to offer him a dog bone, he immediately turns his head to the side with his snout in air, and if I do not react quickly enough, then Pickles walks into the other room and sits near the pantry. Glancing or glaring (it's hard to tell) at me to read his mind and provide immediate culinary satisfaction to his discriminatory, albeit fickle, taste buds. Pickles learned early that the pantry holds crackers, chips, cookies, peanut butter, and coconut oil, and as far as he is concerned they are his as he desires.

Currently, I am attempting to decode his beagle brain to figure out what triggers one snack over another. Since no consistency appears to be present, it has become a challenging endeavor on my part...one that I probably will not figure out. What was met with hearty approval ten minutes ago is now cause for Pickles to turn up his nose and look the other way making me feel shameful for even offering up such inferior snacks. I realize that I am partly to blame. Had I never given him anything other than his dog bone he would have been satisfied. Once I started, Pickles felt that he deserved the very best. I finally sat Pickles down and we read from the Bible.

John 1:16
And of His fullness we have all received, and grace for grace.

I reminded Pickles that the fact that he got a dog bone every time he came inside was a treat in itself, and he should be thankful, there are a lot of dogs that don't even get to come into the house, let alone get a treat.

I got to thinking about my own life and how God has blessed me with everything I need and an uncountable number of "extras." How quickly I begin to complain, "Lord, why can't I have a new house?," "I want to travel the world," "I want to be a better fiddle player," "I want, I want." Ungrateful and unthankful.

God has graced me with every single thing I need along with so many extras, and I, being the blinded person I am, turn my nose up, complain, and ask for more.

1 Chronicles 29:13
Now therefore, our God, we thank You and praise Your glorious name.

What a reminder to me to be much more thankful and less ungrateful, being aware of all the things I take for granted. Each morning I get out of bed and go make coffee, a routine I never think about I just do it. If I stop to break it down, the list is endless...

I am thankful for a roof over my head, a soft bed upon which to lay my head, heat during the cold of winter, and air conditioning for hot summer days. I am thankful I am able to get up on my own and have the money to pay the electric so that I can flip a switch to get light. I am thankful that I have clean fresh water and a nice coffee pot. I am thankful for the job I have that made the money that bought my truck that takes me to town to buy coffee............

The list could go on and on for just one small routine in my day. I am embarrassed by how "entitled" even I have become over what seems the mundane.

Matthew 7:12

Therefore, whatever you want men to do
to you, do also to them, for this is the Law
and the Prophets

Super Bowl

Knowing that there would be a couple of cute dog commercials playing during the super bowl, I decided to allow Pickles to watch some of the Super Bowl last year. Of course, he would not be allowed to watch any of the half time show, as he is much too easily influenced, and one never knows what may or may not happen during the half-time show.

Pickles appeared to enjoy the action on the field, intently following the football. His excitement escalated, however, during the tackles. He's a dog, so I really did not foresee any possible consequences it could create for me by letting him watch part of the game. How wrong I was. The very next day I am strolling across the yard when "wham" I am tackled from behind and nearly rolled across the driveway. I carefully shook Pickles off my leg only to be tackled again. I am talking about a small beagle running at full speed (which Mr. Brown has clocked at 25 MPH) and using his front paws to grab me around the leg. His speed, combined with the inertia of his leap, turns him into a small, lethal torpedo. If that doesn't do the trick, he grabs a long stick and tries to run between my legs, thereby whacking me on both legs at the same time. Pickles thought it was fun, I did not think it was fun. Someone was going to get hurt, and I suspected it would be me. I explained to Pickles that there is a time and a place for football, but he needed to be aware of the time and make sure that others want to play as well.

God wants us to have fun, but not at the expense of someone getting hurt, either physically or mentally. We need to be mindful of others.

I got the Bible down and we read together

Ecclesiastes 3:1-8

1 To everything there is a season, A time for every purpose under heaven:

2 A time to be born, And a time to die; A time to plant, And a time to pluck what is planted;

3 A time to kill, And a time to heal; A time to break down, And a time to build up;

4 A time to weep, And a time to laugh; A time to mourn, And a time to dance;

5 A time to cast away stones, And a time to gather stones; A time to embrace, And a time to refrain from embracing;

6 A time to gain, And a time to lose; A time to keep, And a time to throw away;

7 A time to tear, And a time to sew; A time to keep silence, And a time to speak;

8 A time to love, And a time to hate; A time of war, And a time of peace.

So powerful is this Bible passage that it was the inspiration for a popular rock song, "Turn, Turn, Turn," that became a hit for The Byrds in 1965.

After reading the Bible passage and listening to the rock song version, I began to think about my own life. I thought of the times when I had been happy and light-hearted, wanting to joke and carry on when others around me were sorrowful and heavy-hearted, lacking the ability to be joyful and happy. Were they going through a real heartache and I had failed to show respect and concern for their feelings? Or did I, during my own heavy-hearted days, miss an opportunity to set aside my burdens to put a smile on someone's face?

I really need to be more aware of other's feelings and remember there is a time and place for everything under the heavens. More so than that, I need to be less about me and more about others, putting aside myself. Glen Campbell had a hit country song titled "Less of Me" with the following phrase in the song, "Think a little more of others and a little less of me." Great advice from a country song.

Romans 12:15
Rejoice with those who rejoice, and weep with those who weep.

The Veterinarian

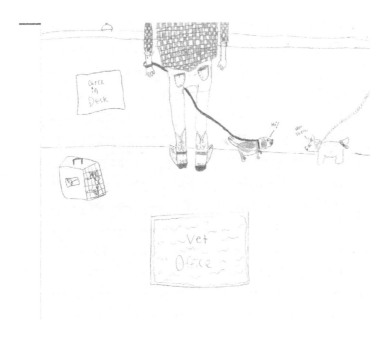

Recently while I was shopping at the local big box store, my attention was drawn to a little chap who appeared to be about four years old. This little guy was throwing a good old-fashioned kicking, screaming, hitting, hissing, flailing and biting fit, one that you could not ignore. The entire store was aware of the young man, and people were retreating to the furthest corner, causing a pile-up in aisle eleven. It was the type of fit that, if it had been me back in my younger days, would have gotten me dragged by the hair of my head to the parking lot where I would have quickly and efficiently had my attitude adjusted. The little guy's mom was clearly flustered and had totally lost all control, with the little rug rat having gained the upper hand. My first thought of course was, "Wow, what a brat, clearly that mom needs to get a grip and regain control of junior. If she can't control him now when he's four, what will he be like as a teenager?" I then proceeded (with a little tilt of my nose in the air) to the farthest corner of the store away from the situation and continued on my merry way, thankful that I didn't have to deal with anything like that.

A few days following this incident, Pickles was scheduled for a follow-up appointment with the veterinarian to see how he was healing up from his recent broken rib incident. The car ride to the Veterinarian's office was uneventful, as Pickles sat in the back seat by himself counting cars as they passed by. I never heard so much as a bark, whimper, or growl out of him. He was the perfect passenger.

Upon securing a parking spot and getting the car parked,

Pickles cheerfully hopped out, trotting so nicely beside me up the sidewalk towards the front door of the veterinarian's office. Providing me with false assurance of good behavior on his part. As we neared the door, however, Pickles threw on the brakes and locked up as sullen as a Missouri Mule. No way was Pickles going to walk nicely in through those doors. After a bit of murmuring and threatening, I managed to shuffle him around, hang on to my purse, push and shove from behind, and get him through the doors.

Immediately upon entering the building, Pickles was face to face with the nastiest, ugliest, old alley cat I have ever laid eyes on. For the safety of everyone in the building, the old tabby was confined to a wire cage with reinforced rebar welded on the corners. This cat clearly meant business. He was hissing and spitting while stretching his arm out of the cage with what appeared to be 6-inch claws. He was swatting at everything and everyone, shredding the air in the process... typical cat behavior in my opinion. The entire population of the waiting room had their backs flattened against the wall in a desperate attempt to avoid being slashed into mincemeat. Pickles was smart enough to realize he did not want to get anywhere near that cantankerous old tabby and kept tucked as close to me as possible, shoving me to the forefront while he hunkered behind me. As luck would have it, the old tabby had just finished up and was soon out the door. Sighs of relief echoed through the waiting room in perfect harmony. We were now free to relax and take up occupancy in the nearest chair.

Suddenly, a small flick of a tail in the far corner captured Pickles' attention, keeping him captivated, with the old tabby quickly becoming nothing more than a mere memory. Pickles' gaze had fallen upon a cute and dainty Australian Shepard mix laying there just oozing that Aussie charm. From Pickles' reaction, it was quite evident she was the most beautiful and charming dog he had ever laid eyes on. The building could have been on fire with a lobby full of hissing alley cats and Pickles would not have noticed. He could not take his eyes off the little Aussie. Pickles commenced to barking, whistling, howling, jumping, and gyrating (Elvis Presley would have been proud). He would stop at nothing to get her attention. She merely blinked in quiet disdain. At this point, I casually asked her owner her age, as it was apparent to me (or so I thought) that she must be quite elderly due to her quiet, laid-back demeanor. The owner casually replied (while looking with disgust at Pickles, I might add), "Seven months." I'm pretty sure I saw a smirk cross that young punk's lips as I replied, "Wow, she's very well behaved," all while being jerked in circles by Pickles. Speaking quietly, he responded, "We start training our (with a strong emphasis on "our") dogs at a young age."

To say that I was humbled and embarrassed would be a major understatement. My cheeks flamed red and I wanted to crawl under something, but it was all I could do to maintain my balance with Pickles' leash wrapped tightly around my ankles. Thankfully, at this point, the little Aussie and her punk kid were called to the back. I was finally able to unwind the leash from my ankles and rub them hard enough to restore blood flow. I finally succeeded in getting Pickles to settle down when in shuffled this short, unsavory-looking, ill-mannered, nondescript breed of dog with uneven legs and scraggly, stiff tufts of hair that jutted out in odd directions. His left eyebrow was higher than the right, with an unkempt scruffy little-dog mustache that seemingly ran uphill. To be honest, I'm pretty certain this was the same dog whose mutt shot I saw in the paper last year as the first-place winner in the ugly dog contest. I decided Pickles must have really bad eyesight, as once again he got all excited and was wagging his tail so hard I was beginning to chill due to the rapid air movement. At this point, it seemed as if we had been waiting in the reception area for an eternity when in reality it was more like 3 minutes. It was a welcome relief to finally get called to the back and into a private room. The first thing the veterinarian noticed was that Pickles' tail was bleeding, to which I quickly replied, "He did that wagging it against the chair leg. He will be okay." Lucky for me, the visit was quick and Pickles received a clean bill of health. I couldn't help but jump up and down as we were released from any further follow-up visits.

As we made our way back to the front of the office and the waiting room I was praying that there would be no other dog or cat encounters between the front door and my car. My prayers were answered, and I was able to pay Pickles' bill and head home.

The moment we arrived back home, Pickles was out of the car and running the neighborhood. I am pretty sure he wanted to go tell his friend Noah about the cute little Aussie at the veterinary clinic.

Later that evening, when Pickles meandered back home, I sat him down, and got the Bible. We read about proper behavior in public and self-control, none of which Pickles had exhibited. I explained that he was so focused on everything around him that he had forgot about me, the one holding his leash. I was the one that should have been in charge.

Proverbs 25:28
Whoever has no rule over his own spirit is like a city broken down, without walls.

When we lose self-control, we lose control of common sense, manners and what is appropriate, of course satan is standing close by to take control and help us out. Not only had Pickles lost control, he lost all concept of reality and his surroundings. When one loses self-control, anything can happen. Our eyes and mind have suddenly lost focus on what is important, everything around us has faded into the background and our brains go to mush.

I know there have been times when I have lost self-control and acted irrationally. The sad part is I acted and said things in a very unchristian manner, things I would not have said had I remained under control. After regaining control, all I can do is hang my head in shame and ask for forgiveness, all while wondering how I could have let such a thing like that happen. I briefly took my eyes off what was important, focusing instead on my own selfish desires.

Wham, I was suddenly out of control, not thinking or acting rationally. How merciful God is, not only forgiving but totally wiping it away never to be remembered.

Isaiah 43:25
I, even I, am He who blots out your transgressions for My own sake; And I will not remember your sins.

I love that last line, "And I will not remember your sins". A promise to forgive and forget. I do pretty good at forgiving, however, I have a great memory that likes to remember things I need to let go.

Suddenly, my mind was drawn back to that little boy I had observed at the store that was giving his mom fits and how I had judged her as failing in her job as a mom.

Luke 14:11
For whoever exalts himself will be humbled, and he who humbles himself will be exalted.

Ouch, believe me, I was humbled by Pickles' behavior at the veterinary clinic. I'm sure God looked down upon my predicament and chuckled.

James 4:10
Humble yourselves in the sight of the
Lord, and He will lift you up.

Top Dog

While reading the news headlines on the computer this morning, I saw the following headline, "Top Dog Breeds in Each State." I was instantly intrigued and made the mistake of casually mentioning it to Pickles, who was immediately up in my face wanting to read it for himself. Of course, I didn't expect to see beagles listed anywhere but naturally, Pickles was certain beagles would be on the list. One by one, I went through all the states reading the results. Wasn't I shocked to read that beagles made it to the top 3 in 10 states (but not Missouri), thus making them in the top 3 overall? Pickles, of course, was delighted and got a little pompous on me, which really wasn't a surprise.

Having the knowledge of beagles that I have garnered from Pickles, I have formulated my own thoughts on the subject. For what it's worth, here is my theory on it all...beagles are marathon runners, running the equivalent of multiple marathons daily. Most of these marathons seem to be ran in somewhat of a straight pattern, resulting in beagles eventually crossing state lines. All those marathon-running beagles are counted in every state they are merely running through. Official beagle counters are not realizing they are actually counting "out-of-staters" and those same beagles will again be counted in the next state in which they are observed (running no doubt). Thus, the straight-line running gives the appearance of more beagles than actually exist. I was proud, however, of Pickles for believing in his ethnicity, and I was not going to be the one to burst his little, bouncy beagle bubble with my analogy. He has a strong faith in his heritage, believing in the "beagle-hood" when even I couldn't believe it (still don't).

Pickles and I sat down later, and I explained that while it is good to believe something you hear, it needs to be checked to make sure it's accurate. The same statistics can prove an argument on either side, depending on how it is presented. If you don't believe me just ask anyone who has taken a college statistics class.

I find it easy in my life to get excited over something I hear (that goes along with my moral and spiritual values) and not think about checking the source. I have seen first-hand how the media has distorted facts to present their beliefs in a positive way. I cannot be too careful in accepting what I hear as the truth. I must check and test the source. I then read to Pickles from the Bible.

1 John 4:1-6
1 Beloved, do not believe every spirit, but test the spirits, whether they are of God; because many false prophets have gone out into the world.
2 By this you know the Spirit of God: Every spirit that confesses that Jesus Christ has come in the flesh is of God,
3 and every spirit that does not confess that Jesus Christ has come in the flesh is not of God. And this is the spirit of the Antichrist, which you have heard was coming, and is now already in the world.
4 You are of God, little children, and have overcome them, because He who is in you is greater than he who is in the world.
5 They are of the world. Therefore they speak as of

the world, and the world hears them.

6 We are of God. He who knows God hears us; he who is not of God does not hear us. By this we know the spirit of truth and the spirit of error.

We are living in a time where we cannot be too careful, and I know, for myself, I need to question and make sure that what I am being told or taught lines up with the Bible. satan is the great deceiver and will stop at nothing to cause us to stumble, even presenting himself as an angel of light.

2 Corinthians 11:14
For satan himself transforms himself into an angel of light.

It does not matter what man says, the ultimate authority is God, and His word stands yesterday, today, and tomorrow.

True Gift

Weather permitting, Mr. Brown and I enjoy drinking our morning coffee on our balcony overlooking the yard. This early morning ritual is one of our favorite times of the day. Some mornings are spent in silence as we absorb God's blessing on and in our lives, other mornings we engage in delightful banter (small talk mainly). This particular morning was no different as we observed Pickles sniffing around the yard in his morning routine, as he takes note of several rabbits conveniently located throughout the yard, any one of which could provide him with a great morning rabbit chase. We all know, however, that the grass is greener and the rabbits run faster on the other side of the fence, something which Pickles is also aware of. Sticking his nose up in the air and tail straight up, Pickles proceeded up the driveway at a moderate beagle pace. Mr. Brown yelled, "Pickles get back here!" Pickles, of course, completely ignored us just as we had expected he would.

What Pickles didn't realize when he left was that Penny, Daffy, and Trixy (his out-of-town dog friends) were coming for a visit a little later in the day. A few hours later, Pickles' friends arrived and were wondering where Pickles was. As the day wore on with Penny, Daffy, and Trixy hanging out at our house, we all began to wonder if Pickles was coming home. I finally decided I better go retrieve Pickles from whatever porch he was lounging on.

My first stop was Noah's house, and sure enough, there was Pickles hanging out. Pickles was not ready to go home, and there was a small dispute before I succeeded in getting him in the truck and home. Once I got Pickles back to the house and he saw that his friends were here his whole attitude changed. This is nothing new, as his attitude changes moment to moment anyway, and usually not in my favor. The whole group of them immediately began romping, rolling, running, and general dog frolicking. As the pack finally wore down from all the strenuous activity, they turned to chew toys. Penny is about 5 times bigger than Pickles, and she happened to find and grab up one of Pickles' favorite toys. Pickles apparently remembered the run-in he had a few weeks back with the neighborhood cat, and decided against confrontation for the moment. Finally, he is beginning to show a little maturity and to think and reason through sticky situations.

Penny's people and I watched in delight as Pickles went to his beagle bed grabbed up a pillow and brought it straight to Penny. What a cute gesture to offer a trade. Of course, Penny's people thought it was the sweetest thing for Pickles to do, and it did have the appearance of a giving, caring attitude.

However, I happened to know that Pickles does not like that pillow in the least. Penny was not too interested in it either; in fact, she rejected the gift. I let it go for the time being, as it seemed best to not correct things with company here.

Later in the evening after Pickle's company had left and things had quieted a bit, Pickles and I sat down to discuss things, and I read to him from the Bible.

2 Corinthians 9:7-8

7 So let each one give as he purposes in his heart, not grudgingly or of necessity; for God loves a cheerful giver. 8 And God is able to make all grace abound toward you, that you, always having all sufficiency in all things, may have an abundance for every good work.

I explained to Pickles that he had not really given anything; he gave something he didn't treasure in his heart. Pickles didn't want that pillow, it had no value to him. Then I got to thinking about myself and my giving and how I often fall short especially in "giving of my time." So often I know I need to spend time helping someone, but I put it off until I have (in my mind) cleared off my own "to do" list. I haven't really given anything, I just got caught up on the things I felt were more important to accomplish. I have a lot of improving to do in that area. I also was reminded of the greatest gift given...God's only Son, Jesus. The ultimate gift from the heart, nothing held back. How it must have hurt God to give the one and only "true gift" and have His Son rejected. It's a good reminder that I need to be more generous with my giving and appreciative of all the blessings I have received. Anyone can give, but to give something you hold dear is to give from the heart.

Watermelon Rind

One of the sweetest things about summer is eating a bright red, sweet, ripe watermelon while the juice runs off your chin and stains your newest white t-shirt (right next to the coffee stain). Every spring I get anxious and wind up buying a few melons that are tasteless and certainly not ripe, some of which are so bad I return to the store. I just can't seem to wait, even though I know in reality that the melons were picked green, and will in fact taste green.

This year has been no different other than the unripe melons seem to have been far more unripe and disappointing than in the past. Finally, this past weekend I hit the watermelon jackpot and secured a perfectly ripe watermelon. I bought it from one of those little road side stands that had a sign out front that said "World's best watermelons". It was pretty close to being one of the best melons I have ever tasted. Now, I am not the type of person that has to chill their watermelon before consumption. I am perfectly content to munch on a room temperature melon, and, as I found out, so is Pickles. The little guy loves watermelon, maybe more than me. So it was with the "World's best watermelon" that Pickles and I shared a little melon munching moment...a beagle-bonding time for Pickles and me. You have to understand also that I am not a traditionalist either when it comes to slicing my melon, nor am I hesitant about eating directly out of the center of the melon. It is after all my watermelon to eat as I wish. With that being said, I had sliced the tip of the melon off, and Pickles and I consumed that slice along with a substantial amount of the "heart" of the melon. I added a couple new watermelon stains to my white t-shirt, and

Pickles had a puddle of watermelon juice on the floor (thankfully tile) where he was snacking. Every bite was worth the t-shirt stain and the prospect of a late night floor mopping.

I have always loved watermelon, but until about 5 years ago I was very cautious about excessive consumption. A family tragedy that happened in 1920 but was mentioned quite often kept my munching in check. It seems a young family member (8 years old) had died in 1920 from "eating too much watermelon". No one ever questioned the cause of death and no other details were known. This was all we were told about the young boy's untimely death. I have to admit that these are the sort of tales that make a major impact on a child's thought process, especially when you have heard the story since you were a youngster. Every bite of watermelon I ate was always with the thought in my head, "How much is too much? Is this gonna be it for me?"

Relief and freedom to eat watermelon in excess came a few years back while I was working on some family history. It happened to be during watermelon season so I felt it would be a good time to uncover the truth. Would the death certificate reveal the youngster's untimely demise was indeed too much watermelon or would I be freed from family fable? I took a deep breath as I munched on my watermelon preparing for the truth, whatever it may be. My hands shook as my eyes scanned the faded death certificate. Sudden relief flooded my whole being as I read the cause of death and saw that he had passed away from a completely different issue. It was a comforting peace and assurance to find that I could now safely consume large quantities of watermelon without fear of it being "too much".

So it was, after considerable melon munching on my part, with Pickles keeping up with me, that I grabbed up the remaining rinds and took to the hill side and flung them into the woods. I know there is wildlife that will enjoy what little is left on the rinds, and I am happy to share.

The following morning, I am on the balcony happily sipping my coffee when I notice Pickles coming up the hill with something in his mouth that looks similar to a Frisbee. As Pickles gets closer, I can tell it is the bottom end of the watermelon rind. Every bit of the red is gone leaving only the white fleshy part. I casually call out his name and ask, "Where are you going?" It is at this point that he looks up, gets all sneaky acting, slinks around to my garden, and hides out with his watermelon rind. I don't know what was going through his beagle brain, but seriously, he is sneaking off with a watermelon rind. I would have been happy to give him a piece from the center of the melon if he would have barked. I went out later to try and locate the rind, but it was nowhere to be found. Either he ate rind and all, or he has it buried somewhere on the "Brownstead", most likely in the middle of the green bean patch. I brought Pickles in later and we read from the Bible.

Matthew 7:7-8
Ask and it will be given to you; seek, and you will find;
knock, and it it will be opened to you.
8 For everyone who asks receives, and he who seeks
finds, and to him who knocks it will be opened.

I explained to Pickles that I would gladly have given him a good piece of watermelon had he asked, but he had decided to be all sneaky about it. It was then that I began to think about my own life. When I decide I want or need something, instead of going to the source, I resort to my own methods of obtaining it, which usually don't work out too good. I wind up with the rind when I could have had the heart if I had only asked God. Does God give me everything I ask for? Thankfully, no, He doesn't. God knows just how much is enough and how much is too much. God wants the absolute best for His children, but sometimes we let our own selfish desires get in the way. God always gives "the heart," and in return God wants our hearts.

Romans 8:38-39

38 For I am persuaded that neither death nor life, nor angels nor principalities nor powers, nor things present nor things to come,
39 nor height nor depth, nor any other created thing, shall be able to separate us from the love of God which is in Christ Jesus our Lord.

Trixy

I remember quite well that look on Pickles' face when he first laid eyes on Trixy nearly 2 years ago. His eyes spoke a million words, most of which were "Will you spend the rest of your life hunting rabbits with me and rolling in cow pies?" Trixy wanted no part of that lifestyle as most of her previous 12 years had been outdoors in the ever-erratic Missouri weather. After her original owner died, she had hit the jackpot and was now living indoors like a queen. It was a rags to riches story of sorts.

Trixy was a once-in-a-lifetime dog, one that could melt the hearts of the heartless. To meet Trixy was to love Trixy. She was a bouncy, bubbly,dainty type, who was forever grateful for every belly scratch, ear rub, or kind word. I don't believe I have ever met a more grateful, happy dog (unlike Pickles who feels he is entitled to everything).

Pickles never gave up, and on Trixy's numerous visits, he would inquire if she had changed her mind. She had not. Thankfully, Pickles is easily distracted, so a throw of a stick, a tuft of hair attached to some bones, a frog, turtle, or anything to be exact, and his mind was off Trixy and he was on his merry way.

Trixy developed some health issues indicating her time here was limited. Her family did everything they could to keep her happy, pain free, and comfortable. Even at her worst, Trixy did not complain and remained grateful. When it became apparent that she would not be getting better and her health had deteriorated to a point she was suffering, the difficult and heart breaking decision was made to let her go. It would be selfish to keep her here for our pleasure.

Mr. Brown and I knew that Trixy's family wanted her brought back to the farm, as some of her happiest moments had been here at the Brownstead. I made the 3 hour round trip to pick her up and bring her back for the last time. Mr. Brown stayed behind and carefully picked out and prepared a final resting place for Trixy. After we had said our final good byes and paid our respects, I sat Pickles down and we read from the bible.

John 3:16

For God so loved the world that He gave His only begotten Son, that whoever believes in Him should not perish but have everlasting life.

I explained to Pickles that as much as we loved Trixy and were saddened by her death, God's love for us is infinitely more. God could have chosen any manner to redeem us, and to cleanse us of our sin, but God wanted us to understand his vast immeasurable love for each of us. Each one of us have lost a loved one, and I'm sure would have done anything possible to keep them. Likewise, God also could have chosen any other means, but, His love prevailed. Jesus' death was brutal. He was publicly humiliated, scorned, mocked, scourged, and hated. God gave His only Son to all mankind, even those who mock Him, hate Him and deny Him. This is proof of a love that not one of us can truly comprehend. God's love knows no bounds, and has no limits. Salvation is free to every man and woman who is willing to accept His free gift.

2 Timothy 4:17
But the Lord stood with me and strengthened me, so that the message might be preached fully through me, and that all the Gentiles might hear...

Isaiah 40:31
But those who wait on the Lord shall renew their strength; They shall mount up with wings like eagles, they shall run and not be weary, they shall walk and not faint

A Beagle and a Bible

As far back as I can remember, about 7 minutes give or take, I have had the ability to arrange common, unheard of, and obscure words in a creative manner with an artistic flare. Some of my ramblings, however, have been misunderstood and reported as graffiti by overly sensitive English majors. At this point in my life, I don't foresee much improvement in my unique word arrangements, and I consider it to be the gift God gave me to reach out to those around me. I also inherited a strong dose of tongue-in-cheek humor from my dad. For these reasons, I was not too surprised when God called me to write *Pickles' Parables*. After all, God does have a great sense of humor, and I'm fairly certain He chuckled to himself as he watched me struggle to deal with Pickles.

My first thought when I felt God calling me to write this book was... *Okay, I can do that. Most of the material is already written, it just needs fluffed up a bit here and there. I'll edit what I have and throw it out there.* Wrong, God made me slow down to His time, give a 100%, and make this book the best that it could be. How presumptuous of me to even consider "just throw it out there". God gave me His everything when He gave Jesus to die for my sins. How could I offer anything less than my very best. God also knew I would need motivated and fed on my journey, so He strategically placed good inspirational books in my path. One of my of my favorites has been, *So God made a dog, 90 devotions for dog People.* Of course satan was quick to point out that these were indeed great books, unlike *Pickles' Parables*, which he assured me was terrible, as well as a waste of time and paper.

In thinking back, I would probably consider May 2012 as "the" beginning. It was during this time that our youngest daughter, Marcy, got married, and Mr Brown and I were "the chosen". Chosen to dog-sit, or pooch pamper in this case, while Marcy and our newly acquired son-in-law Dan were honeymooning. Daffy, a cute, petite, girly girl dachshund lived a sheltered and pampered city life. It was a harsh contrast to the two weeks she was going to be spending in the country. The Brownstead provided a lot of new experiences for a little city dog. During Daffy's stay with us, she managed to get into quite a bit of mischief. I took pictures and wrote short little stories which I then posted on Facebook for Marcy and Dan to see as they traveled the countryside. Daffy was an instant hit on social media. It was at this point that I began to feel a stirring of my spirit to write a book, which at that time seemed absurd to say the least. Fast forward two years, 2014, another haphazard writing episode intensified the stirring of my spirit to write. I had begun to pray for my Facebook friends the first day of every month. Then I began writing and posting a quick message on Facebook saying, "Hey, I'm praying for each of you today." As time went on, I began to not only let my friends know I would be praying for them, but I also included a short devotional as well. The positive feedback I received from those short devotions was unexpected and humbling. More often than not, the devotionals I felt were not well written were the very ones that seemed to speak the most to hurting people. It was proof that God's hand was truly in control of my writing. Shortly after starting these devotionals, I began to receive comments from people saying, "You need to put these in a book." Although I shrugged it off at the time, the seed had been planted.

The final piece fell into place during a trip to visit with our daughters. The route we take passes directly by a large flea market that is very active from early spring to late fall. Mr. Brown is unable to pass by without stopping. It was the perfect June day when we made that fateful stop. The stop that would forever change our lives with the acquisition of the main character. A flea market in a small town in southern Missouri, one small beagle, and *Pickles' Parables* began.

As we made our way past the various vendors selling an eclectic assortment of junk (none of which we needed, I might add), we passed a couple selling beagle pups from the back of a pickup truck. I quickly walked on by. No way did I want a dog, even a cute beagle was out of the question. Mr. Brown paused and lingered a little too long and was sucked in. It wasn't long before I was handed a cute, innocent-looking, little beagle pup and Mr. Brown remarked, "I thought you might need a little company around the house." Not once do I recall mentioning that I was getting lonely, nor did I think a beagle was the answer if I was lonely.

The beagle was with us a month before we found the perfect name. Up until that time, nothing seemed to fit. I posted a few photos of him online so friends and family could give me name suggestions. Then, I started my summer pickling project. This pickling project is a short, but intense, time of canning spicy dill pickles. A typical pickling season will see me canning approximately 100 quarts in about a three week time frame. So it was, that during the height of my 2016 pickling season, it seemed only appropriate that the beagle be named Pickles. Pickling and Pickles, double trouble, one for a short time, and one perhaps for a lifetime.

Now it so happens that as a young girl I raised beagles and enjoyed each and every one of them, each puppy having their own distinct personality. I realize now that as a child I had no other worries, so perhaps that in itself made beagle ownership much more enjoyable. Not so with Pickles. Pickles was, and still is, a very different beagle. I don't recall any beagle I ever owned that has been as difficult, stubborn, independent, and rough-playing as Pickles. There were many nights I went to bed in tears from an evening of bites and nips, with blood (mine) being involved. Perhaps the hardest were those nights when Pickles went outside after dark and did not return until the next day, causing me to lose sleep worrying about him, but also reminding me, that I was to trust God with all things, including this one small beagle.

During this adjustment period that first year, I started posting short comments about Pickles and his latest escapades on Facebook. I needed an outlet to relieve the frustration he caused me, and humor seemed to help. More often than not, I would include a picture of Pickles and his latest antics. Pickles was an instant celebrity. It was only natural that my postings soon turned into a short story with a spiritual lesson or parable. My Facebook friends fell in love with Pickles and soon deemed him the underdog with me being labeled the mean beagle owner. Everyone was rooting and cheering for Pickles in his latest adventures. More than that, were those who were blessed by a particular parable at a time when they needed it most. On those weeks when I seemed to get discouraged, God would send someone to encourage me to continue writing about Pickles. These encouraging moments, and words, were always unpredictable, random, and typically from a source that I would not have expected. It was further proof that I was on the path that God wanted me to be on.

In the spring of 2017, I began to feel God calling me to quit work to concentrate on *Pickles' Parables*. I, of course, was very reluctant to give it up and, in fact, tried to bargain with God. Of course, I knew in my heart that I would never find peace until I fully submitted to God's calling on my life. This step would also prove to be a financial challenge for Mr. Brown and I, as well as a real test of our faith and obedience. Dreams and plans we had would have to be put on hold for now. God has a way of convincing one that His way is always best, and by late fall I knew without a doubt that I needed to be obedient. All that was left was for Mr. Brown to hear the same message (at this point, I had not told him that I felt it was time to quit). In the late fall Mr. Brown felt the calling, responded in obedience, and told me, "It's time for you to quit work, you have a book to write" and that, my friends, was the beginning.

I knew going into this project that satan would try every trick to discourage and defeat me. I was, however, unprepared for how relentlessly hard satan would work.

The drastic means he would go to in order to create roadblocks and prevent the completion of *Pickles' Parables*. It was during those "wordless days", filled with discouragement in which I struggled to write even one word, that God would intervene and send an encourager. I also had many lessons to learn along the way... compassion, trust, timing, and becoming less judgmental towards others. Lessons that often were painful, but in order to grow spiritually they are often necessary. How callous of me to think I was just writing a book.

January 1, 2018, I awoke with excitement and anticipation for this new adventure in my life as an unemployed author. Unable to see the ending, but stepping out in faith. Little did I know at the time, how bumpy my journey would be with physical, spiritual, and mental battles to be overcome. Battered and bruised along the way, yet still blessed beyond what I deserved. Left with scars as a reminder of what God brought me through. Above all, learning compassion and patience for others as I realized each and everyone of us is fighting a battle, some quietly and secretly and some more evident and visible.

1 Peter 3:8
Finally, all of you be of one mind, having compassion for one another;
love as brothers, be tenderhearted, be courteous

Romans 12:15
Rejoice with those who rejoice, and weep with those who

With all of the *Pickles' Parable* material written, it was time to begin the difficult task of editing. Editing, I found out, would take twice as long as it had taken to write the book. This book is God's book, and, as such, I need it to be the best I can humanly get it. After many redos, all the editing was finally done. I was delirious with excitement, thinking I was nearing the end. I was suffering delirium alright, the tough part was just beginning. Formatting. That word deserves to be in a sentence all by itself. Most authors, I have since found out, hire someone to do their formatting, which I would gladly have done. However, God made it clear that I was to do my own formatting. At that point, I didn't know what I didn't know that I needed to know. Formatting a book has been one of the most frustrating and challenging things I have ever tackled and accomplished. I was often angry and questioned God, "If you want me to do this, why is it so hard?" Through many trial and errors, I was finally able to grasp some basic concepts and a book began to take shape. On those days that I made progress in page set-up and formatting, a smile would light up my whole face as I thought to myself, *Wow, I did that, I figured it out, learned something new, and accomplished what I set out to do.*

God continued to provide the knowledge just as I needed it, not before... proving once again that I can trust his perfect timing. So much has been opened up to me during the course of this project, I could not begin to explain or to even write it all down. I have taken it day by day, word by word, with God leaning over my shoulder pointing out words and sentences that needed changed, deleted, or reworded.

Had I been assigned *Pickles' Parables* project years ago, I would not have had the discipline to wait and listen for God to speak, nor could I have clearly seen the parallels. It is only after raising our two daughters and leaving the work force that I was able to give my full attention to the project at hand. I will not deny the fact that there were days I grumbled and did not want to do what seemed to me an impossibility. It was then that I was quietly reminded that Jesus knew beforehand the rejection, pain, and suffering that would be required of Him, yet He loved each of us enough to walk boldly forth, submit to God's will, and lay down His life in a brutal manner as atonement of our sins. When I would begin to worry, fret and get anxious, which was about 85% of the time, God would gently remind me that Pickles and the *Pickles' Parables* belong to him. I know that Pickles is special in his own difficult way and has been sent for the inspirational purpose of writing *Pickles' Parables*.

Romans 5:8

But God demonstrates His own love toward us,
in that while we were still sinners, Christ died for us.

This I know, what I can't do, God will do through me. I must remain open and receptive to His divine plan for my life. This is not as easy as it sounds, but I know in my heart that God always has the best plan for each of us..

Matthew 19:26
"...with men this is impossible but with God all things are possible."

Proverbs 16:3
Commit your works unto the Lord and your thoughts will be established.

The most important part of *Pickles' Parables*, of course, was pulling together the spiritual lesson and finding the right scripture. It was during those scripture searches that I would often weep as I read God's word. Overwhelmed by the power of God's Holy Word, I felt my own spiritual life grow as I spent time studying the Scripture. This was a miracle and blessing in itself. As I searched and read the scriptures, I gained a new understanding of God's infinite love for each of us, a love so strong He chose to give His only Son as a sacrifice for our sins.

This has been a journey requiring 100% faith, especially on those days (of which there were many) when I had no clear directions other than, "One word at a time." Fighting the dark and potentially defeating thought of, *How can I ever complete a project of this magnitude?* Being given the knowledge to complete the assigned project as I needed it, not before. Always being reminded that a book is written one word at a time and through listening intently for the Holy Spirit to guide and direct God's words to my fingertips. A willingness to not ask how or why but to take each individual word, sentence, paragraph, and chapter as God gave them to me. Not looking to the end result, but embracing *Pickles' Parables* day by day, one word at a time. A time to embrace and enjoy the days when the words came easily, a time to grow in faith and reliance upon God's leading on those days when nothing seemed to come easily. A time to slow down and accept God's perfect timing and the blessings along the way.

To this very day, I continue to stand in awe of the impact one small misbehaving beagle has on so many people. Perhaps one of the most humbling, bittersweet moments occurred when Mr. Brown and I were attending the funeral of a family member. As I walked up to offer my condolences on the passing of his wife, he was quick to greet me with, "How's Pickles, are you keeping him in line?" A gentle reminder to me, of what Pickles and his shenanigans have meant to others. Providing laughter and tears, proving once again that God often use's the most unlikely.

I pray that you will be blessed by one or more of the Parables, that there will be one special Parable that will speak to your heart or perhaps put a smile on your face when you are down.

Proverbs 17:22
A merry heart does good
like medicine.....

If you are not saved and have not given your heart to God, I encourage you to do so. God's forgiveness is a gift, free to each and everyone who asks.

Admit you are a sinner.

Believe in Jesus, his virgin birth, death on the cross and his resurrection.

Confess your sins and ask for forgiveness.

I believe that Jesus Christ was born to Mary, a virgin. God, in the human flesh, living on earth, experiencing the same things that we do: sorrow, heartache, joy, happiness, hunger, and pain. When Jesus grew up, He was falsely accused, beaten, and nailed to a cross as all the sins of the world were upon Him. He knew beforehand all the things that He would go through, yet even knowing what He would suffer, Jesus' love for each of us was, and still is, so strong that He was willing to embrace death and take it all. He rose from the dead, defeating even death. His blood covers our sins. One cannot be good enough or do enough. It is only by His grace.

Ephesians 2:8
For by grace you have been saved through faith,
and that not of yourselves; it is the gift of God

Remember, do not look to your fellow man as mankind has a sinful nature. Man will always stumble, mess up, disappoint, and let you down. God will never let you down. I was a sinner now I'm saved by grace. Not perfect but forgiven.

Who knew that one little beagle's adventures, given a Biblical parallel, and shared on social media, would result in a book? God knew.

Hebrews 13:20-21
20 Now may the God of peace who brought up our Lord Jesus from the dead,
that great Shepherd of the Sheep, through the blood of the everlasting covenant,
21 make you complete in every good work to do his will, working in you what is well and pleasing in His sight, through Jesus Christ, to whom be glory forever and ever. Amen.

It has been individuals like those of you that are reading this book (I hope anyway) that provided the courage I needed when I felt defeated. You probably thought nothing of it when you told me how much you enjoyed reading about Pickles. Yet without those encouraging words I would not have been able to continue on. God clearly used so many of you as a source of inspiration, and for that, and for each of you, I am thankful.

If God asks of you, He will walk with you every step of the way. No task is too large or too difficult.

From The Doghouse

The author, Diane Brown, is my mom. She is a wife, mother, grandmother, and friend to many. Mom writes a monthly online devotional that is enjoyed by her friends. She also writes about me (Pickles), which is way more entertaining than that other stuff she writes, and has written several songs as well. Mom has been owned by many beagles in her life, though none have been as cute, or smart, as I am. When she is not busy attending to my various needs and demands, she can be found playing fiddle, attending bluegrass festivals, singing and playing music at nursing homes, pulling weeds from her garden, sipping coffee with dad (Mr. Brown) or searching the neighborhood for me. Mom and dad are also guilty of leaving me from time to time as they go visit their four grandchildren or their ever-changing number of granddogs. They live on The Beaglestead, my farm in Mid-Missouri, which she affectionately refers to as The Brownstead.

Pickles

1 Thessalonians 5:28
The grace of our Lord Jesus Christ
be with you. Amen.

For speaking engagements, book signings or other questions, the Author may be contacted via email at:

picklesparables@gmail.com

Pickles' Parables is available through Amazon, or directly from the author.

Made in the USA
Monee, IL
18 January 2021